DISCARD

GREAT FOOD,
ALL DAY LONG

MAYA ANGELOU

GREAT FOOD, ALL DAY LONG

COOK SPLENDIDLY, EAT SMART

 RANDOM HOUSE | NEW YORK

Published in the United States by Random House,
an imprint of The Random House Publishing Group,
a division of Random House, Inc., New York.

Random House and colophon are registered trademarks of Random House, Inc.

Interior photographs: Brian Lanker

Library of Congress Cataloging-in-Publication Data

Angelou, Maya.
Great food, all day long : cook splendidly, eat smart / Maya Angelou.
p. cm.
ISBN 978-1-4000-6844-9
eBook ISBN 978-0-679-60437-2
1. Cookery, American.   I. Title.
TX715.A5696 2010
641.5973—dc22   2010017519

Printed in the United States of America on acid-free paper

www.atrandom.com

2 4 6 8 9 7 5 3 1

First Edition

Book design by Jo Anne Metsch

I dedicate the ambitious intent of this book to those who would love to eat and love to lose weight at the same time.

While I cannot assure that these recipes will reduce the reader's size, I can say I have tried to offer flavors and savors which will be long remembered and always remembered with a smile of satisfaction.

Miss Dearieo, I hope this will be of use to you.

Contents

Introduction

Some people buy cookbooks just to read, with no intention of trying the recipes. I hail their discipline, because it is impossible to put on weight just reading about food, even if the accompanying photographs cause the salivary glands to dance wildly in the mouth.

And there are those who want to lose weight, so they choose to read books about dieting, swearing a fierce loyalty to the books' recipes and suggestions. There are those who say they would cook if they had the time, or the skills, but since they don't, they delight in reading what serious cooks are able to create. Only a few readers buy cookbooks to really cook the recipes. If this book finds its way into the hands of bold, adventurous people, courageous enough to actually get into the kitchen and rattle the pots and pans, I will be very happy.

I started working on this book over a year ago, and in that time I have eaten from all the recipes described here. I treated myself to delicious dishes, some from my childhood and others I had encountered in travels around the world. I studied cookbooks diligently and was particularly influenced by the writers who loved food, who were gourmets but not gourmands. M.F.K. Fisher, Elizabeth David, Jessica Harris, Margaret Visser, and Jacques Pepin are among the cooks and writers whose work encouraged me.

I read that if a diner ate only a small portion of food, and waited twenty minutes, she would be surprised to find that the small amount she had consumed satisfied her hunger—that is, if the food was really savory, really tasty. Because I live alone, I knew it would be easy for me to follow that advice on portion control. If I chose to roast a chicken, I *could* plan to eat at least four meals from it. I am sure that if I had to sit at a table with my family, I would find it more challenging to eat only a little—though not impossible. The cook in the family can prepare a sumptuous meal for the family's enjoyment and still employ portion control, knowing that it's okay to return two or three hours later and, without guilt, have a little more.

I found that when I ate a few barbecued ribs and a serving of a few vegetables, I could set the rest aside and return to it later. Likewise, a piece of buttered toast and two soft-boiled eggs would successfully break my fast and fuel me for my morning's labor, or were light enough to be consumed at night without fear of indigestion and nightmares. I only noticed that I was losing weight when my clothes began to appear noticeably too large.

I put the two together and deduced that portion control was the secret to my weight loss.

Some years ago I found my health in danger because I was over-weight. My doctors warned me that I was dangerously close to diabetes, hypertension, and high blood pressure. I tried any number of diets, some silly and some lugubriously serious. Nothing worked for very long. But since I enjoy food, am a good cook, and am well into my upper age group, I decided there must be a way to take the pounds off and keep them off. I made some changes and lost thirty-five pounds. I diminished my portions, and ate more frequently. The title of this book, *Great Food, All Day Long,* came from that exercise. I eat less, but more often, and the foods I create are wondrously flavorsome.

Most people on our planet live without cereal or even any knowl-edge that there are foods meant solely to be eaten during mornings and others for lunch and yet others for dinner. People the world over eat in the morning some of the leftovers of what they had at dinner the night before.

As I prepared to write this book, I thought of dishes that would be as good at 8:30 p.m. as they were at 8:30 a.m. I have not suggested cereal or eggs as the only breakfast foods. With my recipes you can have fried rice for breakfast, lunch, or dinner. All recipes offered in this book can be prepared and eaten all day long, beginning with a glorious chili. You can have couscous with chicken drumsticks any time of the day or night. The food should taste so good that you will be satisfied with a small portion. If you are diligent about portions, then you can snack with smaller amounts all day long.

I have not tried to cut calories by creating fat- and sugar-free dishes, although I have been careful in not overdoing those foods. I use butter, olive oil, and even lard—sparingly, but enough so that the diner can taste the flavors and be satisfied.

I hope that you will find these recipes delicious and fulfilling. I hope that portion control will come easier because of the delight that you will find in these dishes. And finally, I hope you will agree with the philosopher who said "less is more."

A BRAND-NEW LOOK
AT OLD LEFTOVERS

My mother dreamed that one day we would together compose a cookbook. In her dream I would cook the entree, then she would take what was left and show how it could be prepared in such wonderful ways that the family would not have any inkling that they were being served leftovers.

We spent glorious afternoons and after-dinners imagining the wonderful dishes that could be created by adding just a few more ingredients. We imagined that a dish first served as a roasted entree would be very different if it appeared as a refried or boiled offering.

This book begins with three principal dishes and the glorious creations that can be made from them.

CROWN ROAST OF PORK

1. Preheat the oven to 375°F.
2. Sauté the apples and prunes in the butter in a skillet over low heat.
3. After 3 minutes, remove the skillet from the heat and set the prunes aside in a separate dish. Let cool.
4. Mix the garlic, thyme, oregano, salt, and pepper with the olive oil until you have a paste. Rub the paste into the meat.
5. Place the meat in a shallow roasting pan and bake for 30 minutes.
6. Reduce the oven temperature to 325°F and roast for 2 hours.
7. Remove the roast from the oven once the internal temperature reads 165°F on a meat thermometer.
8. Place 1 prune on each rib and return the meat to the oven for 20 minutes.
9. Remove the meat from the oven, and put the rest of the cooled fruit into the center of the crown roast.
10. Place 1 pork chop carved from the roast and 1 tablespoon of apples onto one plate for as many servings as necessary. Refrigerate the remainder.

SERVES 8. Serving size: One pork chop and 1 tablespoon of apples.

3 apples, peeled, cored, and cut into large dice
8 dried pitted prunes
1 tablespoon butter
1 teaspoon granulated garlic
1 teaspoon dried thyme
1 teaspoon dried oregano
½ teaspoon salt
¼ teaspoon pepper
1½ tablespoons olive oil
8 pounds pork ribs (have butcher fashion into crown roast)

If you would like to give a grand dinner party, plan to serve this crown roast of pork. Be prepared for the admiring "oohs and ahhs" that will fill the air. Remember, cooking a large amount of food does not mean that you are obliged to eat large portions.

CREAMY PORK HASH

1 medium onion, diced

2 tablespoons vegetable oil

One 10¾-ounce can cream of
mushroom soup

½ cup frozen peas

½ cup frozen sliced carrots

1 cup diced cooked potatoes

2 cups cooked pork roast
(page 5) cut into medium
dice

1 cup water

½ teaspoon salt

½ teaspoon pepper

1. Sauté the onion in the vegetable oil in a skillet.
2. Add the cream of mushroom soup, peas, carrots, and potatoes.
3. Add the pork and thin the mixture with the water.
4. Add the salt and pepper.
5. Cover the skillet and simmer for 15 minutes.
6. Serve 2 heaping tablespoons on a dinner plate. Refrigerate the remainder.

SERVES 4. Serving size: 2 heaping tablespoons.

Pork Tacos

1. Dampen each tortilla with ½ teaspoon water, and cover with a paper towel.
2. Place in a microwave oven for 10 seconds on high power, then remove.
3. Place 2 tablespoons pork on one side of a tortilla.
4. Add 1 teaspoon cheese, 2 teaspoons lettuce, 2 teaspoons tomatoes, and 2 teaspoons salsa (and onion, if desired) to each tortilla.
5. Fold the tortillas over, covering the meat and toppings completely. Tortillas can also be fried in canola oil, 1 teaspoon for each.

SERVES 4. Serving size: 1 taco.

4 corn tortillas

2 teaspoons water

4 thin slices cooked pork roast , shredded by hand or using two forks

1 cup shredded Monterey Jack cheese

2 cups shredded lettuce

1 cup tomatoes cut into large dice

2 cups tomato salsa

½ medium onion, thinly sliced (optional)

4 teaspoons canola oil (optional)

This is one of my favorite dishes to go back to. Within three hours, I'm almost always ready for a second taco. And given the generous quantities listed in the ingredients, you'll definitely have more waiting for you.

PORK FRIED RICE

1. Whisk together the soy sauce and 2 tablespoons water in a small bowl until blended. Set aside.
2. In a large nonstick skillet, sauté the chopped onion, scallion tops, and garlic in 1 teaspoon of the oil on moderate heat. Fry until soft and translucent.
3. Remove the onion and garlic mixture to a bowl and set aside.
4. In the same skillet, heat ¼ teaspoon of the oil, beat the eggs, and fry until cooked through completely, tilting the pan so that the eggs evenly cover the bottom.
5. Remove the eggs from the pan and set aside. Once cooled to room temperature, cut the eggs into ½-inch ribbons.
6. Heat the remaining 1 teaspoon oil in the frying pan. Add the diced pork, the rice, mushrooms, and soy mixture, and cook until heated completely. Add the onion and garlic mixture and egg ribbons. Stir thoroughly, and serve immediately.

2 tablespoons soy sauce

1 medium onion, chopped

3 medium green scallion tops, chopped

2 garlic cloves, minced

2¼ teaspoons canola oil

2 eggs

1 cup cooked pork roast cut into small dice

2 cups cold cooked rice

One 8-ounce can sliced mushrooms, drained

SERVES 4. Serving size: 1 cup.

PRIME RIB
The Dinner That Never Stops Giving

Marinade

1 teaspoon granulated garlic

1 teaspoon kosher salt

¼ teaspoon black pepper

2 teaspoons Italian
    seasoning

1 teaspoon lemon pepper

2 tablespoons olive oil

1 teaspoon French's Classic
    Yellow Mustard

5 ribs prime roast of beef

½ cup black coffee (optional)

1. For the marinade, mix together the garlic, salt, black pepper, Italian seasoning, lemon pepper, olive oil, and mustard. Stir well until the ingredients are blended into a smooth mixture.

2. Spread the marinade over the meat, covering it completely.

3. Wrap the meat loosely in aluminum foil and refrigerate overnight.

4. About 1 to 2 hours before ready to prepare, remove the meat from the refrigerator and place in a shallow roasting pan, ribs down. (The ribs will act as a rack.) Allow the roast to come to room temperature.

5. While the roast is sitting, preheat the oven to 400°F.

6. Put the roast into the oven and cook for 20 minutes.

7. Insert a meat thermometer into the densest part of the meat. Turn the oven down to 340°F and cook for 1½ hours or until the temperature reaches 165°F for medium. (For well done, cook for an additional hour or until the temperature reaches 180°F; for more rare, reduce the cooking time to 1 hour or until the temperature reaches 140°F.)

8. Remove the roast from the oven and let sit for 20 minutes before carving. Carve and serve.

9. Once finished serving, remove the remaining meat from the bones, wrap the meat and bones separately in aluminum foil, and refrigerate.

10. Pour the leftover drippings into a saucepan and remove the fat. Add the coffee if you like. Salt to taste. Mix well. You now have a *jus*.

SERVES ABOUT 12. **Serving size: One 4-ounce slice.**

OPEN-FACED SLICED BEEF SANDWICHES

1. Remove the meat from the refrigerator and slice into 4 thin slices about 1 ounce each. Return the remaining meat to the refrigerator.
2. Prepare the gravy: Combine the beef stock and cornstarch in a bowl. Add salt and pepper to taste.
3. Pour the gravy into a skillet and add the sliced meat. Heat the meat in the gravy over low heat for 10 minutes.
4. On each of two plates, place 2 thin slices of sandwich bread. Place 1 tablespoon of gravy on each slice. Place one slice of beef on each of the 4 slices of bread. Cover with 1 to 2 more tablespoons of hot gravy.
5. Serve with coleslaw on the side, if desired.

SERVES 2. Serving size: 2 thin slices of beef on 2 slices of bread.

Cooked prime rib (page 12)
2 cups beef stock
1½ tablespoons cornstarch
Salt and pepper
4 thin slices sandwich bread
2 tablespoons coleslaw (optional)

ROAST BEEF HASH

1 pound cooked prime rib
(page 12)

1 tablespoon canola oil

1 medium onion, diced

2 celery stalks, diced

1 white potato, peeled,
boiled, cooled to room
temperature, and diced

1 cup beef gravy (see page
13, gravy for sandwiches)

Salt and pepper

3 poached eggs (optional)

1. Dice the prime rib into medium pieces.
2. Heat the oil in a skillet. Add the onion and celery, and sauté until translucent.
3. Add the potato and meat to the sautéed onion and celery and cook for 6 minutes.
4. Add the gravy to the skillet and heat for 5 minutes.
5. Season with salt and pepper to taste.
6. Serve with poached eggs, if desired.

SERVES 3 GENEROUSLY. Serving size: 3 heaping tablespoons of hash and 1 poached egg.

BEEF AND VEGETABLE SOUP

1. Put 2 quarts water and the beef stock in a large pot.
2. Add the meat, bones, onion, bay leaf, and garlic.
3. Bring to a boil, then turn down the heat and add the carrots, potato, tomatoes, corn, and peas. Let simmer slowly for 1 hour.
4. Remove the soup from the heat, and remove the bay leaf and the bones.
5. Bring the soup to room temperature, and skim off the fat.
6. Add salt and pepper to taste.

SERVES 6. Serving size: 1 medium bowl.

1 quart beef stock

1 pound cooked prime rib, diced, plus reserved bones (page 12)

½ medium onion, diced

1 bay leaf

3 large garlic cloves, minced

2 medium carrots, peeled and diced

1 white potato, peeled and diced

One 28-ounce can crushed tomatoes

One 15-ounce can whole kernel corn

One 8-ounce package frozen peas

Salt and pepper

ROASTED CHICKEN

Juice of 1 lemon, plus one lemon for slicing, if desired

One 8-pound roasting chicken

2 tablespoons (¼ stick) butter

½ teaspoon salt, or more if desired

½ teaspoon pepper, or more if desired

1 unpeeled Granny Smith apple, cored and cut into pieces

1 celery stalk, cut into medium-size pieces

½ cup chopped green lettuce

1. Preheat the oven to 350°F.
2. In a small cup, mix together the lemon juice and 1 cup water. Set the lemon aside.
3. Wash the chicken in the lemon juice mixture. Pat dry.
4. Rub the butter over the chicken.
5. Liberally salt and pepper the chicken outside and inside.
6. Place the apple and celery in the chicken cavity. Place the chicken in a roasting pan.
7. Place an extra-large piece of aluminum foil over the chicken, leaving a generous air pocket over the top of the chicken so the foil does not touch it. Crimp the ends of the foil to the sides of the pan, creating a tent.
8. Bake the chicken in the tent for 1½ hours, partially removing the tent periodically to baste with pan juices.
9. Remove the foil and reduce the oven temperature to 325°F. Bake the chicken, uncovered, for 30 additional minutes.
10. Once the chicken is done (when the internal temperture reaches 160°F), remove the skin and slice for serving.
11. Serve with simple lettuce and garnish with a very thin slice of lemon, if desired.

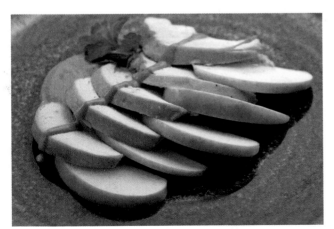

SERVES 6. Serving size: 2 slices of breast.

A chicken breast is less caloric than chicken thighs, but one chicken thigh, skinned, can be considered a serving.

CHICKEN TETRAZZINI

1. Bring 3 quarts of water to a rolling boil in a large pot. Add the pasta and let boil until cooked to desired tenderness. Drain and set aside.
2. In a large skillet, heat the oil over medium-low heat. Add the onion and sauté until translucent.
3. Add the garlic powder, white pepper, and flour to the skillet and cook for 2 minutes, stirring frequently. Be careful not to let the mixture brown.
4. Add the mushrooms, chicken, stock, cream, and salt and black pepper. Stir well to completely cover the chicken.
5. Cover and let cook for 15 to 20 minutes over low heat.
6. Serve over the cooked pasta.

SERVES 4. Serving size: ½ cup pasta, ½ cup chicken.

8 ounces dried pasta (thin spaghetti or angel hair recommended)

2 tablespoons vegetable oil

1 medium onion, sliced into slivers

1 teaspoon garlic powder

½ teaspoon white pepper

2 tablespoons all-purpose flour

5 oyster mushrooms, slivered

2 cups roasted chicken (page 16) shredded by hand or using two forks

2 cups chicken stock

½ cup heavy cream

1 teaspoon salt

1 teaspoon black pepper

CHICKEN CURRY

1. Sauté the onion in the oil in a medium-sized skillet, until translucent; do not brown.
2. Add the curry, cumin, ginger, and bay leaf to the onion and cook for 5 minutes.
3. Add the chicken, the stock, and the salt and pepper, and cook for 10 minutes. Remove bay leaf.
4. Serve with hot white rice or rice pilaf, if desired.

SERVES 4. Serving size: 2 heaping tablespoons of curry over 1 cup of rice.

Relishes such as raisins, mango chutney, cashew nuts, or avocado can be offered with the curry.

1 small onion, sliced

1 tablespoon canola oil

4 teaspoons medium-hot curry powder

1 teaspoon ground cumin

½ teaspoon ground ginger

1 bay leaf

2 cups diced roasted chicken (page 16)

1 cup chicken stock

1 teaspoon salt

1 teaspoon pepper

4 cups cooked white rice or rice pilaf (optional)

PALATE APPETEASERS

eenagers may differ in ethnic, racial, cultural, and economic backgrounds—African American, White American, Asian, Latino, and Native American—but there is one area where they are alike: They all love hot dogs. The flavor of the wiener, the choice or choices of mustard, relish, ketchup, or sauerkraut may vary, but young palates are satisfied with the simple everyday hot dog.

I confess that on certain days, a similar yearning also comes over me, and I can only be satisfied with a loaded hot dog. That said, my palate has had the opportunity to develop some sophistication.

Take, for instance, moo goo gai pan. When my son, Guy, was six, we would often dine at a little Chinese restaurant in San Francisco. Their moo goo gai pan—chicken wings boiled and rolled in a batter with sesame seeds, and fried—was Guy's favorite, and because he loved it so much, I learned to make it.

I've also come to like red tripe, which is tripe cooked with red tomatoes, onion, and garlic and served over steamed white rice. I do make a very good duck liver pâté with truffles, and mustard greens with ham hocks, which can make a person cry for his grandmother, but . . . back to the hot dog.

When I make a chili, I always put about a quart away in the freezer in half-cup portions. Weeks or months later, long after the chili has first been served, I will get a hot dog bun, a Hebrew National wiener, prick it with a fork, broil it for a few minutes, and split it. Then I heat up the chili, put one half of the split hot dog on the bottom piece of bun, and put one heaping tablespoon of chili on the hot dog. I put away the other half for later. Next, I scatter a teaspoon of diced raw onion onto that concoction, then open an ice-cold beer and pour half of it into an ice-cold mug.

At that moment I will not only not answer the telephone, I will not respond, even if my name is called by someone who knows me well.

Chili Guy

1. Sauté the onion and garlic in the vegetable oil in a medium-sized heavy pot until translucent.
2. Add the ground round and pork. Cook until the meat is cooked all the way through, about 15 minutes, stirring frequently.
3. Add the oregano, thyme, sage, cardamom, chili powder, salt, black pepper, and cayenne pepper and cook for 3 more minutes.
4. Add the tomatoes and tomato paste, and stir until all the ingredients are mixed together well. Cover and cook over medium heat for 20 minutes.
5. Add the beef stock or water, cornmeal, and rinsed pinto beans, if desired, and stir.
6. Cover and reduce the heat, and simmer for 1 hour.

SERVES 4 TO 6. Serving size: 1 cup of chili over ½ cup of rice.

This recipe would be sufficient for 4 to 6 hearty diners. It also serves a party very well. If your party is larger, double or triple the recipe as needed. If you have leftovers, let them cool, place in zippered bags, and freeze to be used at a later date (with a hot dog!).

1 medium onion, chopped

2 garlic cloves, chopped

¼ cup canola oil or other vegetable oil

1 pound coarse ground round

⅓ pound ground pork

½ teaspoon dried oregano

½ teaspoon dried thyme

½ teaspoon dried sage

¼ teaspoon ground cardamom

2 tablespoons chili powder

¼ teaspoon salt

⅛ teaspoon black pepper

¼ teaspoon cayenne pepper

One 6-ounce can whole tomatoes, chopped into medium pieces

Half an 8-ounce can tomato paste

2 cups beef stock or water

3 teaspoons cornmeal

One 15-ounce can pinto beans, drained and rinsed (optional)

Steamed rice (optional)

Santa Fe Chili with Meat

2 pounds boneless beef chuck, cut into 1½-inch cubes

½ cup all-purpose flour

2 large onions, chopped

3 garlic cloves, minced or crushed

½ cup olive oil or other vegetable oil

Red Chile Sauce (page 29; optional)

2 tablespoons minced fresh cilantro

2 teaspoons ground cumin

¼ teaspoon ground cloves

1 teaspoon crushed dried oregano

1½ teaspoons dried rosemary

1½ teaspoons dried tarragon

Two 28-ounce cans whole tomatoes and their liquid

2 cups homemade chicken stock or one 14½-ounce can low-sodium chicken or beef stock

1. Sprinkle the beef with the flour in a bowl and mix together. Set aside.
2. In a 6- to 8-quart pot, cook the onions and garlic in the oil over medium heat, stirring often, until the onions are soft, about 10 minutes.
3. Add the meat mixture and Red Chile Sauce (if desired) to the pot. Cook, stirring constantly, until the meat begins to brown, about 5 minutes.
4. Add the cilantro, cumin, cloves, oregano, rosemary, tarragon, tomatoes and their liquid, and stock. Simmer, uncovered, until the meat is very tender, about 1 hour, stirring often.

SERVES 4 TO 6. Serving size: ½ cup of chili over ½ cup of rice.

For a more flavorful dish, cook and refrigerate for up to 2 days, and reheat before serving. Or place in zippered bags and freeze to be used with a hot dog at a later date. And for a spicier kick, add more Red Chile Sauce (page 29) to taste.

Red Chile Sauce

1. Stem and seed the chiles and combine with 3 cups water in a 2½- to 3-quart pot.
2. Cover and simmer over medium-low heat until the chiles are very soft, about 30 minutes.
3. Remove the chiles from the pan and place them in a blender, saving the cooking water.
4. Puree the chiles, adding cooking water as needed, until you have a very smooth mixture, about 3 minutes.
5. Pour the sauce through a fine strainer, rubbing firmly, into a container. Discard the residue.
6. Add the sauce to chili or other dishes as desired.

4 ounces (12 to 15) dried pasilla chiles (New Mexico or Anaheim chiles work best)

Spicy Barbecued Spareribs

1 teaspoon salt

½ teaspoon pepper

2 pounds baby back
spareribs, cut into serving
pieces

1 cup chicken stock

Barbecue Sauce

½ cup vinegar

2 tablespoons honey

⅓ cup ketchup

1 teaspoon powdered
mustard

½ teaspoon paprika

Dash of hot pepper sauce

1 garlic clove, minced

½ teaspoon salt

¼ teaspoon black pepper

1. Preheat the oven to 350°F.
2. Stir together 1 teaspoon salt and ½ teaspoon pepper. Sprinkle over the spareribs and rub in thoroughly. Place the coated ribs in a shallow roasting pan.
3. Pour the chicken stock over the ribs and place the ribs in the oven. Cook for 1½ hours or until tender.
4. Meanwhile, prepare the barbecue sauce. Mix together the vinegar, honey, ketchup, mustard, paprika, hot pepper sauce, garlic, and the remaining ½ teaspoon salt and ¼ teaspoon pepper in a small saucepan. Simmer over low heat for 15 minutes.
5. Remove the spareribs from the oven and place them in a broiling pan. Brush the spareribs with the barbecue sauce and return to the oven on the lowest rack. Set the oven to low broil, and broil the spareribs for 30 minutes, brushing frequently with the sauce. To tell when they're done, pierce the meat between the bones with a fork. If the fork comes out easily, the meat is done.

SERVES 4. Serving size: ½ pound of ribs.

IS VARIETY FINE CUISINE?

Many years ago I was invited to be a distinguished visiting professor at Wichita State University. I taught there for four weeks while staying with family friends.

My hosts, Dr. and Mrs. George Rogers, had two daughters and the first microwave I had ever seen. The daughters were very clever teenagers, who cooked everything they could find in the microwave oven.

I elected to cook some special dishes for the family. I prepared a beef bourguignonne one night, and a beef stroganoff a few days later. On a Sunday I cooked curried lamb and served it with mango chutney, cucumber, cashew nuts, raisins, and diced tomatoes.

While the adults enjoyed my creations, the young ladies could barely choke them down.

My husband, Paul, visited from California for a weekend, and he offered to cook his version of a London grill. He fried steak, liver, bacon, a beef kidney, and pounds of sliced onions in butter. The Rogers girls loved the fried dinner. They ate bites of everything and then as we sat around the table, they said, "We know who the real cook is in your family, Auntie Maya. Your meats were okay, but the gravies were horrible, and it took you so long to cook everything. Uncle Paul has come and within an hour he has us all sitting at the table eating a gourmet dinner."

I kicked Paul under the table.

This is a great meal to serve a large party of carnivores. There is something within this mélange to satisfy any and every palate, and since the meats are sliced in strips 1 inch thick and 2 inches long, everyone can sample everything without overeating.

When I was young, my mother would watch young women pay our butcher sixteen dollars for two half-pound cuts of filet mignon. She then would pay the butcher thirty-two dollars for the whole beef loin, from which she could get twelve hearty steaks and eight to ten cuts of filet mignon. I do the same to this day, and have found that using filet mignon instead of top sirloin adds a touch of sophistication—and succulence—to my London grill.

Mixed London Grill

1. Wash the kidney halves and remove all the veins and fat.
2. Soak in water with ½ teaspoon of the salt for 1 hour and pat dry.
3. While the kidney is soaking, season the bratwurst, lamb chops, pork loin, beef, veal, and livers with pepper and the remaining 1½ teaspoons salt.
4. Grill the pork loin in a grill pan on top of the stove until cooked all the way through. Then grill the kidney, bratwurst, lamb, beef, veal, and liver until medium done. Set aside in a warming dish.
5. In a large skillet, fry the bacon until crispy, turning frequently. Remove the bacon and add to the dish with the grilled meats.
6. Return the skillet to the stove, and fry the onions in the oil.
7. Mix all the meats and the onions together and put over low heat for 5 minutes or until all are warm and cooked through.
8. Serve on a warm platter with a 1-inch-thick slice of grilled or toasted sourdough bread.

SERVES 6. Serving size: 1 spoonful of onions, 1 forkful of each meat, 1 slice of bacon, and ½ slice toasted bread. Be careful with portions, and be discreet. You can always go back.

1 lamb or veal kidney, halved

2 teaspoons salt

1 whole bratwurst or other sausage

2 lamb chops

2 thin slices pork loin

2 pounds top sirloin, sliced

2 pounds veal cutlets, sliced

2 pounds calves' livers, sliced

¼ teaspoon pepper

8 strips bacon

½ pound onions, sliced

2 tablespoons vegetable oil

Shepherd's Pie

¼ pound fatty bacon, finely chopped

1 pound ground beef

1 garlic clove, chopped

2 shallots, chopped

1 medium onion, chopped

1 tablespoon chopped fresh parsley

2 tablespoons tomato paste

2 tablespoons dry white wine

1 teaspoon salt

½ teaspoon pepper

1¾ pounds potatoes, peeled and cubed

3¼ tablespoons butter, cut into small pieces

⅛ teaspoon ground nutmeg (optional)

½ cup grated cheddar cheese

This dish is especially filling and satisfying when served with a romaine lettuce salad with vinaigrette.

1. In a large skillet set over high heat, cook the bacon until crisp and remove to paper towels to drain.
2. Fry the beef in the bacon fat.
3. Add to the beef the garlic, shallots, onion, parsley, tomato paste, wine, and ½ teaspoon of the salt and ¼ teaspoon of the pepper.
4. Simmer over low heat, partially covered, for 30 minutes, stirring occasionally.
5. While the beef is simmering, boil the potatoes in water in a medium-sized saucepan with the remaining ½ teaspoon salt until tender, about 2 minutes.
6. Drain the potatoes and mash, mixing in 2 tablespoons of the butter.
7. Season with the remaining ¼ teaspoon pepper, and the nutmeg, if desired.
8. Preheat the oven to 450°F. Use ¼ tablespoon of the butter to coat the bottom and sides of a shallow 9 × 13-inch casserole or baking dish.

9. Spread a layer of potatoes on the bottom of the dish. Place all of the meat mixture and bacon on top of the potato layer, and cover with the remaining potatoes.

10. Sprinkle with the cheddar cheese and dot with the remaining 1 tablespoon butter.

11. Bake for 20 minutes or until the cheese is melted and lightly browned and the dish is hot throughout.

SERVES 6 OR 7. Serving size: 3 tablespoons is generous.

Original Joe's Sausage, Eggs, and Greens

2 pounds red or green Swiss chard

2 tablespoons vegetable oil

1 pound mild Italian sausage, casings removed

2 large onions, finely chopped

2 garlic cloves, minced

½ pound mushrooms, sliced

¼ teaspoon ground nutmeg

¼ teaspoon pepper

¼ teaspoon dried oregano

2 cups beef stock

6 large eggs

Salt

1 cup shredded Monterey Jack cheese

1. Rinse the greens well. Cut the chard leaves into thin shreds; thinly slice the stems. You should have about 5 cups, lightly packed. Set the greens aside.
2. Place a wok or 12- to 14-inch skillet over high heat. Add the oil.
3. Crumble the sausage into the pan, stirring frequently until the meat is well browned, about 10 minutes.
4. Add the onions, garlic, mushrooms, nutmeg, pepper, and oregano. Stir often, until the onions are soft.
5. Add the beef stock.
6. Stir in the greens, a portion at a time, until all the greens are in the pan and just wilted, 10 minutes.
7. Beat the eggs lightly in a bowl. Add the eggs to the pan and stir over low heat just until softly set.
8. Season to taste with salt.
9. Transfer to a warm serving dish and sprinkle with the cheese.

SERVES 6 OR MORE. Serving size: 1 cup.

Pytt I Panna
Swedish Hash

1. In a large skillet, heat 3 tablespoons of the oil over medium heat. Add the onions and sauté until soft and golden, about 5 minutes.
2. Using a slotted spoon, transfer the onions to a hot plate, leaving as much oil as possible in the skillet.
3. Return the skillet to the heat and brown the potatoes for 4 minutes. Using the slotted spoon, transfer the potatoes to the plate with the onions, again leaving as much oil as possible in the skillet.
4. Return the skillet to the heat and warm the meat for approximately 3 minutes. Return the onions and potatoes to the skillet and mix thoroughly with the meat.
5. Season with the salt and pepper and heat thoroughly for 2 minutes.
6. In a separate frying pan, add the remaining ½ tablespoon oil, and fry the eggs.
7. Serve the hash on the hot plate, garnished with the fried eggs and sliced cucumber pickles.

SERVES 4. Serving size: 1 cup of hash with 1 egg.

3½ tablespoons canola oil

3 medium onions, diced

3 cups cooked potatoes, peeled and diced

2 cups diced leftover cooked beef

½ teaspoon salt

¼ teaspoon pepper

4 large eggs

Cucumber pickles, sliced

Meat Loaf

1. Sauté the onion and celery in the oil until translucent. Add the breadcrumbs, thyme, basil, and red wine. Remove from the heat and allow to cool for 15 minutes.
2. In a large bowl, combine the cooled mixture with the beef, veal, and pork, mixing well.
3. In a separate bowl, beat together the milk, egg, beef stock, salt, and pepper. Pour into the meat and combine. Cover with aluminum foil and refrigerate for 2 hours.
4. Preheat the oven to 375°F.
5. Remove the meat from the refrigerator and place in a loaf pan, packing firmly.
6. Bake for 1 hour and 20 minutes.
7. Spread the ketchup over the meat loaf and return the loaf to the oven for 15 minutes.

SERVES 6. Serving size: One 4-ounce slice.

2 tablespoons minced onion

½ cup very finely chopped celery

2 tablespoons canola oil

1 cup dried breadcrumbs

¼ teaspoon dried thyme

¼ teaspoon dried basil

½ cup red wine

1¼ pounds lean ground beef

½ pound veal, ground

¼ pound lean pork, ground

½ cup milk

1 egg

1 cup beef stock

1 teaspoon salt

¼ teaspoon pepper

3 tablespoons ketchup

TIP

Shop Well and Cook Well

It is wise for a cook to spend serious money on heavy pots. The same goes for good knives. It is wise for a cook to make friends in a local kitchen store, where there will be news about cooking classes and a good produce market, and where knives can be sharpened.

Sweet-and-Sour Meatballs

1. Combine the breadcrumbs, onion, salt, and pepper with 1½ cups water in a large bowl. Let stand for 5 to 10 minutes.
2. Lightly beat the eggs in a separate small bowl. Add the eggs, ground beef, pork, and tomato sauce to the breadcrumb mixture. Mix well.
3. Shape into small balls (20 to 30).
4. Preheat the oven to 350°F.
5. Heat the oil in a large skillet. Brown the meatballs in the oil. Remove the meatballs to a roasting pan and pour out the fat in the skillet.
6. Combine 1½ cups water and the stock in the skillet. Stir and pour over the meatballs.
7. Cover the roasting pan with aluminum foil and bake for about 20 minutes.
8. Meanwhile prepare the sweet-and-sour sauce. In a large saucepan, combine 4 cups water, the vinegar, brown sugar, and soy sauce and bring to a boil.
9. Thicken with the cornstarch mixed with ¼ cup cold water and cook until the sauce is thick and clear.
10. Remove the meatballs from the oven and pour the sweet-and-sour sauce over them. Return them to the oven for 10 minutes.

SERVES 7 OR 8, Serving size: 3 small meatballs with sauce over ½ cup cooked rice.

¾ cup fine dried breadcrumbs
1 tablespoon instant minced onion
½ teaspoon salt
¼ teaspoon pepper
3 eggs
2 pounds ground beef
1 pound bulk pork sausage
1¼ cups tomato sauce
2 tablespoons vegetable oil
1 cup beef stock

Sweet-and-Sour Sauce
¾ cup apple cider vinegar
1 cup firmly packed light brown sugar
¼ cup soy sauce
½ cup cornstarch

WAKING UP TASTE BUDS

Taste buds are particular and unique to each person. I accept the phrase "It calls for an acquired taste," which allows that upon first meeting a comestible and hating it, over time one can become not only used to it, but desirous of it. I have come to like, and even love, foods that at first sight, I wished to never taste again, see, or have their names spoken in my vicinity.

For instance, I thought that eggplant was a waste not only of the chef's time, but even wondered if the Creator could not have used time to better results. My lack of appreciation was the result of eating an eggplant dish called "poor man's caviar." When I had the good fortune to eat ratatouille, and eggplant Parmesan, I came under the spell of eggplant and I expect to be mesmerized by that vegetable my life long.

There are some dishes that have not caught my fancy yet, but I will not close the door and say I will never order them and enjoy their flavors. In today's world, with the general concern about starvation and obesity, I have discovered that overeating can be countered by making the food savory and by eating small portions throughout the day and evening. The eater will be pleased with quality rather than quantity.

Eggplant Parmesan

1. Sprinkle the salt onto the eggplant in a colander placed in the sink. Let drain for 1 hour. Rinse and pat dry.
2. Heat the olive oil in a skillet.
3. Sprinkle the granulated garlic on the eggplant slices. Dip each slice into the breadcrumbs and fry in the hot skillet for 3 minutes on each side.
4. Remove to paper towels to absorb unnecessary oil.
5. Preheat the oven to 350°F.
6. Place the eggplant in an oiled baking pan.
7. Ladle a teaspoon of tomato sauce onto each eggplant slice and sprinkle with the cheese, covering completely.
8. Bake for 20 minutes or until the cheese is melted and lightly browned. Serve immediately.

SERVES 4 OR 5. Serving size: 2 slices of eggplant.

2 teaspoons salt

1 large eggplant, cut horizontally into ½-inch slices

3 tablespoons olive oil

2 teaspoons granulated garlic

1 cup seasoned breadcrumbs

1¼ cups tomato sauce

¾ cup grated Parmesan cheese

Braised Lamb with White Beans

8 ounces dried white beans, soaked overnight in cold water to cover

1 bouquet garni (1 sprig each thyme and parsley, 1 bay leaf, and 6 cloves tied in a square of cheesecloth)

¾ medium onion, chopped

¾ medium carrot, chopped

1½ pounds lean lamb shoulder, cut into ½-inch-thick slices

½ teaspoon salt

¼ teaspoon pepper

¼ teaspoon sugar

2 tablespoons all-purpose flour

1½ tablespoons vegetable oil

1½ cups dry white wine

¾ tablespoon tomato paste

1½ ripe tomatoes, quartered

3 garlic cloves, crushed

Italian bread (optional)

1. Drain the water from the beans.
2. Cover the beans, bouquet garni, onion, and carrot completely with water in a large, heavy-bottomed saucepan. Cover and bring to a boil, then reduce the heat to low and simmer for 1½ hours.
3. Meanwhile, put the lamb in a large bowl and sprinkle with the salt, pepper, sugar, and flour.
4. Heat the oil in a large skillet, add the seasoned lamb, and brown it over medium heat.
5. Add the beans, bouquet garni, onion, and carrot and their liquid to the lamb.
6. Add the white wine, tomato paste, tomatoes, and garlic. Bring to a boil.
7. Cover and simmer until the liquid has been reduced and all the ingredients are tender.
8. Discard the bouquet garni.

SERVES: 6 TO 8. Serving size: 1½ cups and 1 piece of hot Italian bread, if desired.

Club Steaks with Parsley Butter

4 individual club steaks, about ⅓ pound each

1 tablespoon canola oil

½ teaspoon kosher salt

¼ cup dry red wine

¾ cup beef stock

1 tablespoon butter

½ teaspoon whole black peppercorns

Parsley Butter

2 tablespoons chopped fresh parsley

1 tablespoon butter

This is also delicious cold or sliced into salad greens.

1. Trim any fat from the steaks.
2. Heat the oil in a large skillet over medium heat and sear the steaks in the hot oil, frying for 3 to 4 minutes on each side.
3. Remove the steaks to a warm platter and sprinkle with the kosher salt.
4. Quickly pour the wine into the hot skillet; let it sizzle and reduce by more than half, about 2 minutes.
5. Add the beef stock and continue to boil until reduced to about ⅓ cup. Add the butter and peppercorns, stirring until the butter is melted.
6. Remove the peppercorns to a paper towel. Using a mallet or heavy pan, crack the peppercorns and return them to the skillet. Stir well.
7. Prepare the parsley butter: In a food processor, blend together the parsley and butter until smooth.
8. Spoon the sauce over the steaks and serve with 1 teaspoon of parsley butter each.

SERVES 4. Serving size: 1 steak and 1 cup green salad.

TIP

Flavored Butters

Herb Butter

½ cup chopped fresh basil, or

½ cup chopped fresh thyme, or

½ cup chopped fresh oregano, or

½ cup chopped fresh rosemary.

1 stick butter or margarine, at room temperature

1. Wash the herbs thoroughly and dry thoroughly. Strip the leaves from the stems and very finely chop.
2. Mix the herb of your choice with the soft butter and place the butter on wax paper.
3. Roll the butter into a log and place the log packet in aluminum foil. Roll tightly and place in the refrigerator.

MAKES 1 ROLL OF FLAVORED BUTTER

Garlic-Cilantro Butter

8 tablespoons (1 stick) butter or margarine, at room temperature

½ cup chopped fresh cilantro (coriander) leaves

2 garlic cloves, minced or crushed

Using a food processor, mix the ingredients together.

MAKES ⅔ CUP

These flavored butters can be prepared using other herbs, like dill and marjoram. If you want to serve butter over individual steaks, unwrap the log and cut round pats of butter. Replace the roll in the refrigerator and put 1 pat over each steak as it is served.

Oxtail Stew

1 tablespoon canola oil

2 pounds oxtail, cut into 2-inch pieces

2 to 3 tablespoons all-purpose flour

1 celery stalk, coarsely chopped

½ bay leaf

½ teaspoon dried thyme

3 garlic cloves

2 cups boiling water

6 small carrots, peeled

1 tablespoon minced fresh parsley

½ teaspoon salt

¼ teaspoon pepper

1. Heat the oil in a large heavy skillet.
2. Dredge the oxtail in the flour in a bowl, and place in the skillet. Stir constantly over brisk heat until the meat is seared, about 15 minutes.
3. Add the celery, bay leaf, thyme, and garlic, stirring constantly until brown.
4. Stir in the boiling water, reduce the heat, cover, and simmer for 1½ hours.
5. Add the carrots and parsley and continue simmering for 1½ additional hours or until the meat is tender. Remove bay leaf. Add the salt and pepper.

SERVES 6 TO 8. Serving size: 1 piece of oxtail and 2 tablespoons of gravy.

Scallops of Turkey Breast

1. Slice the turkey breast into 8 scallops.
2. Pat the scallops dry and dust with the flour well seasoned with the salt and pepper.
3. Place between pieces of wax paper and pound each scallop two or three times.
4. Heat the butter and oil to sizzling in a large skillet. Brown the scallops three or four at a time to avoid crowding, turning each when brown.
5. Return all the scallops to the pan and cook for 5 minutes. Remove, set aside, and cover to keep warm.
6. In the same pan, cook the shallots until brown, add the wine, and cook down quickly, scraping up the braised bits.
7. Add the milk and cook the mixture down to a syrupy thickness, creating a sauce.
8. Reduce the heat and return the scallops to the pan with the sauce. (If the sauce is too thick, thin with the chicken stock, adding a little at a time to obtain the desired consistency.)
9. Sprinkle the turkey with the toasted sesame seeds and serve.

SERVES 8. Serving size: 1 scallop.

One 4-pound turkey breast

¼ cup all-purpose flour

½ teaspoon salt

¼ teaspoon pepper

1 tablespoon butter

2 tablespoons vegetable oil

2 tablespoons minced shallots or scallions

¼ cup dry white wine

½ cup skim milk

⅓ cup chicken stock (optional)

¼ cup sesame seeds, toasted

Cabbage Rolls with Sauerkraut and Pork

1. Bring 1 quart of water to a boil with the salt in a medium saucepan.
2. Add the cabbage leaves and boil for 4 to 7 minutes. Drain and dry on paper towels.
3. In a large skillet, sauté the chorizo and onion until the onion is translucent. Remove from the heat and let cool.
4. Season the meat mixture with the pepper and mix with the rice. Place 2 tablespoons of the meat mixture in each cabbage leaf. Roll the leaves and secure with toothpicks or poultry skewers. Set aside.
5. In a clean skillet, layer the sauerkraut and cabbage rolls, beginning and ending with the sauerkraut.
6. Add 1 quart water and simmer for 35 minutes, adding more water if needed.
7. Sprinkle with paprika and serve each roll with a dollop of sour cream.

SERVES 6. Serving size: 1 cabbage roll, with an extra spoonful of sauerkraut.

¼ teaspoon salt

6 large cabbage leaves

½ pound fresh chorizo pork sausage (if dried, remove casings)

1⅓ tablespoons finely chopped onion

¼ teaspoon pepper

1⅓ cups cooked rice

1⅓ cups sauerkraut, thoroughly washed

Paprika

One 8-ounce container sour cream

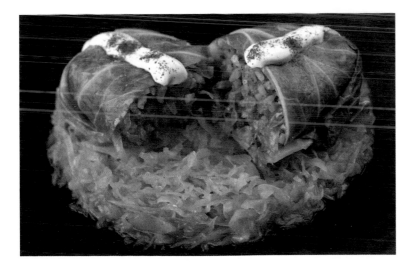

FILLING AND FULFILLING

Childhood stories, fairy tales, and myths have told us that that which we seek may be found at the bottom of fountains, or by rubbing magic lamps, or at the end of rainbows. Princesses—and what girl is not one—have been led to think that they might, just might, kiss frogs and be rewarded by finding handsome princes in attendance.

I have noticed that many people eat long after they are filled. I think they are searching in their plates not for a myth, but for a taste, which seems to elude them. If a person's taste buds are really calling for a prime rib of beef or a crispy brown pork chop, stewed chicken will not satisfy. So the diner will have another piece of chicken and another piece of bread and some more potatoes, searching in vain for the flavor that is missing.

You will note in this cookbook that from time to time I will deliver philosophical announcements. I don't think there is an excuse for that. However, there is an explanation.

At one time, I described myself as a cook, a driver, and a writer. I no longer drive, but I do still write and I do still cook. And having reached the delicious age of eighty-one, I realize that I have been feeding other people and eating for a long time. I have been cooking nearly all my life, so I have developed some philosophies. Maybe some are high flown, but at least I have tested them and found them to the point. I believe that a bowl of savory clear soup served with a corn stick or a slice of irresistible corn bread can be filling and fulfilling. I believe if you will try these dishes together and wait two or three hours before another serving, you will be fulfilled.

Pork Pie

1. Combine the pork, nutmeg, mace, cornstarch, salt and pepper, and 1 cup water in a large bowl. Blend thoroughly with a wooden spoon. Transfer to a skillet and simmer, covered, for 30 minutes, stirring frequently. Once the meat is thoroughly cooked, remove from the heat and set aside to cool.
2. Preheat the oven to 425°F.
3. Pour the meat mixture into the bottom crust in a pie pan. Cover with the remaining pastry and seal the edges with water.
4. Mix the egg and ½ cup water in a cup. Brush the egg wash over the pastry.
5. Prick the sealed pie with a fork to allow steam to escape during baking. Place the pie in the oven and bake for 10 minutes.
6. Reduce the heat to 350°F and bake for 35 minutes longer or until the top is brown.

SERVES 6. Serving size: 1 slice. (Slice the pie into 6 pieces.)

1 pound lean ground pork

¼ teaspoon ground nutmeg

⅛ teaspoon ground mace

2 teaspoons cornstarch

1 teaspoon salt

½ teaspoon pepper

2 frozen 8-inch piecrusts, defrosted

1 egg

TIP

Time Yourself

Plan your meal carefully. If you are cooking meat, remember it will take longer than vegetables, and some vegetables will cook before others. Do not start every dish at the same time.

Mixed-Up Tamale Pie

1. Lightly coat a medium casserole dish with 1 teaspoon of the oil and set aside.
2. Heat the remaining oil in a large skillet. Add the ground beef, onion, tomatoes, garlic, tomato sauce, salt, and pepper. Cover and simmer for 20 minutes.
3. Add the corn, taco sauce, chili powder, and olives.
4. Mix together the cornmeal and 1 cup water in a bowl until smooth. Pour into the skillet with the meat. Stir until all the ingredients are thoroughly combined.
5. Pour into the prepared baking dish and sprinkle the cheese on top.
6. Bake for 50 minutes to 1 hour, until lightly browned on top.

SERVES 6. Serving size: 3 heaping tablespoons. Serve with lettuce salad.

3 tablespoons canola oil

1 pound ground beef

1 medium onion, chopped

One 15-ounce can crushed tomatoes

2 garlic cloves, minced

One 8-ounce can tomato sauce

¼ teaspoon salt

¼ teaspoon pepper

One 15-ounce can whole kernel corn

One 4½-ounce jar taco sauce

2 teaspoons chili powder

1 cup pitted black olives

6 tablespoons yellow cornmeal

1 cup diced sharp cheddar cheese

Veal Chops Supreme

½ teaspoon salt

¼ teaspoon pepper

½ cup all-purpose flour

Four 1½-inch-thick veal chops

2 tablespoons vegetable oil

1 cup sour cream

1. Whisk together the salt, pepper, and flour in a bowl. Coat the veal chops lightly in the seasoned flour.
2. Heat the oil in a large skillet. Add the chops and cook until brown.
3. Preheat the oven to 350°F.
4. Remove the chops and place in a shallow baking dish.
5. Add 1 cup hot water to the skillet and stir in ½ cup of sour cream until well blended. Pour enough over the chops to half cover them.
6. Bake, covered, for 1 hour.
7. Remove the chops from the oven. Stir the remaining sour cream mixture in the skillet and pour over the chops.
8. Cut each chop in half and serve.

SERVES 6 TO 8. Serving size: ½ chop with bone attached with 1 portion of roasted vegetables.

Pollo in Salsa

1. Season the chicken with ½ teaspoon of the salt and ¼ teaspoon of the pepper. Dredge in flour.
2. Heat the oil in a large skillet. Add the chicken and brown on all sides.
3. Remove the chicken onto paper towels.
4. Return the skillet to the heat and brown the onion and garlic in any remaining oil. Add the chili powder, remaining salt and pepper, the bay leaves, and cumin.
5. Mash the tomatoes and cinnamon and add to the skillet. Add the 2 cups boiling water and simmer for 20 minutes.
6. Return the chicken to the skillet and cook until tender, turning occasionally, about 30 minutes. Add more water if necessary to reach the cook's desired thickness. Remove bay leaves.

SERVES 6 TO 8. Serving size: 1 piece of chicken (preferably ¼ breast).

1 frying chicken, cut up
1 teaspoon salt
½ teaspoon pepper
½ cup all-purpose flour
¼ cup vegetable oil
1 medium onion, chopped
2 garlic cloves, chopped
⅛ to ½ teaspoon chili powder
2 bay leaves
½ teaspoon ground cumin
One 28-ounce can whole tomatoes
2 cups boiling water
1 cinnamon stick

Puchero and Corn Bread

1½ pounds beef brisket

1 pound beef short ribs

1 cup all-purpose flour

2 tablespoons canola oil

1 pound kielbasa (Polish sausage)

¼ pound salt pork, sliced

2 garlic cloves, minced

1 teaspoon dried basil

1 teaspoon ground cumin

1 teaspoon dried thyme

1 teaspoon dried rosemary

2 celery stalks, chopped

1 medium onion, chopped

½ teaspoon salt

¼ teaspoon pepper

2 cups beef stock

One 8-ounce can chickpeas, drained

2 medium carrots, peeled and cut into large dice

2 sweet potatoes, peeled and cut into large dice

½ pound pumpkin meat, cut into large dice

1 cup frozen corn

All Day and All Night Corn Bread (page 124)

1. Dust the brisket and short ribs with the flour.
2. Heat the oil in a large skillet. Add the short ribs and brisket and brown.
3. In a large saucepan, combine the sausage, salt pork, garlic, basil, cumin, thyme, rosemary, celery, onion, salt, and pepper. Add enough beef stock to cover all the ingredients.
4. Boil for 20 minutes, skimming any fat from the top.
5. Preheat the oven to 375°F.
6. Add the chickpeas to the saucepan.
7. Remove all the ingredients from the saucepan and place in a large casserole dish with the short ribs and the brisket. Bake for 1 hour and 45 minutes.
8. Put the carrots, sweet potatoes, pumpkin, and corn in the saucepan and cook slowly until tender, about 20 minutes.
9. Remove the casserole from the oven, skim any fat from the top, and adjust the seasonings as desired. Add the contents of the saucepan.
10. Serve over squares of corn bread.

SERVES 10. Serving size: 1 small slice of brisket plus 1 short rib plus 1 slice of sausage over a 2-inch square of corn bread.

Though the meat and chickpea stew known as puchero is widely popular in Spain's Andalusia region and across Spanish-speaking South America, my particular version is inspired by the flavors in the rich Brazilian dish *feijoada*, a pork and black bean soup whose origins can be traced back to the arrival of African slaves on South American shores.

This dish is labor intensive and demands constant attention. However, few dishes will please a crowd more than Puchero and Corn Bread. This stew will serve 10 or more people. If you have more guests, simply add more ingredients—1 more pound of brisket and 1 more pound of frozen corn kernels and 4 more carrots.

Pinto Beans

1 pound dried pinto beans

1 large ham hock

2 garlic cloves, minced

½ medium onion, diced

2 bay leaves

½ teaspoon salt

¼ teaspoon freshly ground pepper

1. Examine the beans, removing any debris, then wash thoroughly. Soak overnight in water to cover.
2. Boil the ham hock for 1½ hours or until tender.
3. Drain the beans.
4. Put the beans, ham hock, and the remaining ingredients in a large saucepan. Bring to a boil.
5. Reduce the heat and simmer about 1 hour. Remove bay leaves.
6. Remove 1½ cups of cooked beans to a large bowl. Mash them with a potato masher until creamy and return to the saucepan. Simmer for another 5 minutes.
7. Serve alone, or with a cup of rice or a square of corn bread.

SERVES 4 TO 6. Serving size: 1 cup.

COOKING VEGETARIAN WITH COURAGE I

ven the most eager meat-eater can have a day when she wants vegetables. I had such a day many years ago. I may have had a surfeit of steaks, chops, sausage, and even jerky. I longed for a plate of greens and a bowl of white rice, or I would have been satisfied with a baked potato and a green salad.

I was living in Los Angeles—where the climate is friendly to new trends—and the vegetarian population flourished. One morning, with my appetite calling for steamed rice and broccoli, I found a vegetarian restaurant called Ye Olde Health Food Diner. Once I had settled in, I gave the waitress my order. "Rice and veggies, please."

At the time I was a smoker, and while I am not proud of that statement, I am happy to report that I have been free of nicotine for over twenty years. But I was a smoker when I entered the restaurant on the day in point. After the waitress took my order, I reached into my purse and took out an unopened pack of cigarettes. I don't know if the rustling of the cigarette paper alerted her or if she had a natural alarm for tobacco, but in seconds she turned and raced back to my table. She bent low and brought her face uncomfortably close to mine. She hissed, "Don't you dare. That is a nasty habit." She added, "Filthy, filthy, filthy." I backed up as far as I could in the booth. Her frown would have frightened a dragon. She said, "You have endangered everybody in this place." Mind you, I had not even pulled the little strand of cellophane from the package.

I looked at the customers at the counter, the tables, and in the other booths and they all looked pitiful, and pale. They had long faces, lank hair, sad, half-dead eyes. I said to the waitress, "I suppose these are all newcomers. They just started coming here to get better."

She drew herself up in a huff and responded, "No, these are vegetarians, they have been coming here for years."

I beckoned to her to come close and I hissed into her ear in a stage whisper, "Don't ever tell anyone that these people have been coming here for years, and are still looking no better than they do now."

My statement made her look at her customers, and in that second, I gathered my purse and my unopened cigarettes and fled the joint. I went home and in self-defense I wrote the following poem:

THE HEALTH-FOOD DINER

No sprouted wheat and soya shoots
And brussels in a cake,
Carrot straw and spinach raw
(Today I need a steak).

Not thick brown rice and rice pilau
Or mushrooms creamed on toast,
Turnips mashed and parsnips hashed
(I'm dreaming of a roast).

Health-food folks around the world
Are thinned by anxious zeal,
They look for help in seafood kelp
(I count on breaded veal).

No Smoking signs, raw mustard greens,
Zucchini by the ton,
Uncooked kale and bodies frail
Are sure to make me run

to

Loins of pork and chicken thighs
And standing rib, so prime,
Pork chops brown and fresh ground round
(I crave them all the time).

Irish stews and boiled corned beef
And hot dogs by the scores,
Or any place that saves a space
For smoking carnivores.

Those sentiments of twenty years ago have given way to my becoming enchanted with vegetables.

I have met and adopted two composers and songwriters, Nick Ashford, who is a strict vegetarian, and his wife, Valerie Simpson, who wavers a bit. I love to cook for them, for they are good food lovers with great palates. I have developed a large number of vegetable dishes for them, which I also love. I have discovered that many of these dishes stand shoulder to hip with meat entrees without shyness or apology. I offer a number of them to you in the pages that follow.

Omelet with Spinach

1. Oil an 8 × 4½-inch loaf pan. Set aside.
2. Heat the tomatoes in 1 tablespoon of the olive oil in a large skillet until the liquid has mostly evaporated.
3. Season with the thyme, salt, and pepper and set aside to cool.
4. Heat the remaining olive oil in a small skillet or saucepan and stir in the spinach. Season to taste with nutmeg.
5. Preheat the oven to 400°F.
6. Break the eggs into a large bowl and beat with an electric mixer.
7. Add the cream and the cheese.
8. Mix the tomatoes and the spinach together and place them in the bottom of the prepared loaf pan. Pour the egg mixture on top.
9. Place the loaf pan in a larger pan half-filled with hot water and place the larger pan in the oven.
10. Bake for 35 to 45 minutes, until the omelet is puffed and lightly golden.
11. Remove the loaf pan from the oven by itself. Run a knife around the edges of the pan to loosen the omelet, and invert the omelet onto a plate. Reinvert the omelet onto a serving platter.
12. Serve hot or at room temperature with a green salad tossed with olives and a bit of olive oil. This omelet will also work well as a sandwich filling.

SERVES 4. Serving size: ¼ omelet.

One 28-ounce can whole
  plum tomatoes, chopped
1½ tablespoons olive oil
¼ teaspoon dried thyme
½ teaspoon salt
¼ teaspoon pepper
1 cup cooked spinach
Freshly grated nutmeg
4 large eggs
2 tablespoons heavy cream
½ cup grated Gruyère cheese

Baked Eggs

4 large eggs

½ large onion, thickly sliced

4 tablespoons (½ stick) butter, melted

1⅓ cups milk

4 teaspoons fresh lemon juice

4 teaspoons chopped fresh parsley

½ teaspoon curry powder

¼ teaspoon ground cumin

⅛ teaspoon red pepper flakes

⅔ cup grated Swiss cheese

⅓ cup grated white cheddar cheese

1. Hard-boil the eggs and remove the shells. Put the eggs back in their water to keep warm.
2. Sauté the onion in the butter in a large skillet for 10 to 12 minutes, until just tender.
3. Pick up the onion in a slotted spoon and remove to paper towels to drain, reserving the drippings for a later use, if desired.
4. Slice the eggs into halves and place, yolks up, in a baking dish.
5. Preheat the oven to 350°F.
6. Mix the onion with the milk, 2 tablespoons water, the lemon juice, parsley, curry powder, cumin, red pepper flakes, and cheeses in a large bowl. Pour over the eggs.
7. Place the baking dish in the oven and bake for 30 minutes.

SERVES 4. Serving size: 1 egg with 1 serving of green salad. (Remember, you can go back in a few hours for seconds.)

Thousand Island Eggs

½ cup sour cream

¼ cup chopped stuffed olives

1 tablespoon chopped fresh
chives

¼ cup ketchup

Pinch of garlic salt

Dash of hot pepper sauce

½ teaspoon salt

¼ teaspoon pepper

4 teaspoons butter

4 eggs

1. Mix together the sour cream, olives, chives, ketchup, garlic salt, hot pepper sauce, salt, and pepper in a medium bowl.
2. Preheat the oven to 400°F.
3. Put 1 teaspoon butter in each of four ramekins or baking cups, and put the ramekins in the oven to melt the butter quickly.
4. Remove the ramekins, and break 1 raw egg into each (the eggs will begin to cook immediately). Pour the sour cream mixture, evenly divided, over the eggs, and place in the oven. Bake for 15 to 20 minutes, until set.

SERVES 4. Serving size: 1 ramekin.

This dish can be cooled and still enjoyed. Simply warm the egg in a microwave for 30 seconds and serve with a few tablespoons of cooked vegetables or a few thick slices of salted ripe tomatoes drizzled with balsamic vinegar. This dish is excellent for a midnight snack, or early morning breakfast.

TIP

Temperature Control

It is wise to make certain foods to be served hot, some to be served at room temperature, and others whose flavor comes through best when they are ice cold.

When serving a dinner buffet-style, arrange to have hot foods served hot from a chafing dish. Be certain that foods you are serving at room temperature are correctly served that way.

Kasha

1 egg, beaten

1 cup kasha

1 teaspoon salt

¼ cup vegetable shortening

1. Combine the egg, kasha, and salt in a bowl, mixing thoroughly.
2. Melt the shortening in a large skillet. Stir in the kasha mixture and 2 cups water. Bring to a boil, then quickly reduce the heat to low.
3. Cook, tightly covered, over low heat for about 30 minutes or until the grains are soft.
4. Serve as you would rice or vegetables, or in soups, or with gravy.

SERVES 3 OR 4. Serving size: 2 tablespoons.

Succotash

1. Combine the ingredients in a large, heavy pot. Simmer, covered, for about 15 minutes over low heat.
2. Increase the heat and cook for 30 minutes more, stirring occasionally. Serve hot.

SERVES 4. Serving size: ½ cup succotash as a side dish.

1 cup lima beans (fresh, frozen, or canned)

1 cup frozen whole kernel corn

¼ cup chicken stock

1 tablespoon butter

½ teaspoon sugar

½ teaspoon salt

¼ teaspoon pepper

Pink Beans

4 cups dried pink beans or small red beans (about 1½ pounds)

2 tablespoons canola oil

1 large Spanish onion, chopped

One 28-ounce can crushed tomatoes

3 large garlic cloves, chopped

2 large carrots, peeled and chopped

3 celery stalks, chopped

2 bay leaves

½ teaspoon salt

¼ teaspoon pepper

1. Sort through the beans and remove any debris. Rinse and drain the beans.
2. Combine the beans and 8 cups water in a 5-6 quart pot. Soak overnight.
3. Heat the oil in a large skillet and sauté the remaining ingredients until the onion is translucent.
4. Drain the beans and add 8 cups water. Bring to a boil, then reduce the heat, cover, and simmer until the beans are tender to the bite, 2 to 2½ hours. Remove bay leaves.
5. Combine beans and vegetables, stirring well. Season to taste with additional salt if needed.

SERVES 8. Serving size: 1 cup of beans with ½ cup white rice.

If made ahead of time, cover and refrigerate. Before serving, bring to a simmer over medium heat, stirring constantly. Serve with white rice and garnish with cilantro.

Southern-Style Green Beans

1. Remove the tips from the beans and break the beans into pieces 1 to 1½ inches long.
2. Wash and dry the beans.
3. Heat the canola oil and olive oil in a large skillet. Cook the sliced onion for 3 minutes.
4. Add the green beans, mushrooms, and salt.
5. Cook slowly, covered, for 30 to 40 minutes, until tender. When the beans are done, there should be very little or no liquid left in the skillet.
6. Serve hot as a main dish or as a side dish.

SERVES 2 AS A MAIN DISH, 4 AS A SIDE DISH. Serving size: 1 cup as a main dish, ½ cup as a side dish.

1 pound green beans

1 teaspoon canola oil

1 teaspoon olive oil

½ medium onion, sliced

1 pound portobello mushrooms, sliced

1 teaspoon salt

California Green Chile and Cheese Pie

1. Preheat the oven to 350°F. Bake the piecrust just until pale golden, about 12 minutes. Remove from the oven and let cool slightly.
2. Reduce the oven temperature to 325°F.
3. Sprinkle the Jack cheese and ½ cup of the cheddar cheese over the bottom of the partially baked crust.
4. Evenly distribute the chiles over the cheese.
5. Beat together the half-and-half, eggs, and cumin, if using, in a bowl, until blended. Pour over the chiles.
6. Sprinkle evenly with the remaining ½ cup cheddar cheese.
7. Bake on a sheet pan or cookie sheet for 40 minutes or until the center of the pie appears set when the pan is gently shaken. Let stand for about 15 minutes before cutting.
8. Serve warm or at room temperature.

SERVES 6. Serving size: 1 slice.

1 frozen single piecrust

1½ cups shredded Monterey Jack cheese

1 cup shredded mild cheddar cheese

One 4-ounce can diced green chiles, drained

1 cup half-and-half or light cream

3 large eggs

⅛ teaspoon ground cumin (optional)

This pie can be separated into 6 slices. Served with green salad, it makes a light yet filling supper.

Corn Pudding

1 tablespoon melted butter

2 15-ounce cans whole
kernel corn

4 eggs

½ cup half-and-half

3 tablespoons all-purpose
flour

½ teaspoon sugar

¼ teaspoon grated nutmeg

¼ teaspoon ground
cinnamon

½ teaspoon salt

¼ teaspoon pepper

1. Using the melted butter, grease a medium casserole dish.
2. Drain the corn as completely as possible.
3. Whisk the eggs together briskly in a large bowl, until blended. Add the half-and-half and continue to blend.
4. Preheat the oven to 350°F.
5. Add the flour, sugar, nutmeg, cinnamon, salt, and pepper to the egg mixture and stir well. Add the corn and mix together.
6. Pour into the prepared casserole dish and bake for 1 hour.
7. Remove from the oven and let cool for 15 minutes. Serve hot as a side dish or as a snack.

SERVES 4 OR 5. Serving size: ½ cup.

Consider the richness of the ingredients. Enjoy a small portion.

COOKING VEGETARIAN
WITH COURAGE II

Hundreds of cookbooks line the walls in my country kitchen. I can sit at the table and reach the books. Since I have read each one at least one time, I do not make a selection. I simply choose whatever book my hand falls on. When I look up, it is to find that my stomach is making unpleasant gurgling sounds, my saliva glands have been hard at work, and two hours have passed.

I rarely follow recipes from one cookbook at a time. I will study three recipes for the same dish to see how three different cooks would prepare the ingredients. I might select ideas from one, and then add my own innovation. The end results are not always successful, but the chances and changes, more often than not, offer a wonderful dish that I doubt any of the original cooks would recognize. Experimenting can breathe new life into vegetable dishes that will satisfy even the most discriminating palates.

Enjoy!

Crudités with Vinaigrette

1. In a large saucepan, boil the potatoes in a quart of salted water until soft, about 20 minutes. Remove the potatoes from the water and set aside.
2. Add the asparagus, broccoli, carrots, peas, and scallions, and boil together for 6 minutes.
3. Remove the vegetables from the pot and rinse in ice water. Drain the vegetables and dry. Peel and cut the potatoes in half, and put them in a large bowl with the other cooked vegetables.
4. Prepare the dressing: In a blender, puree 3 tablespoons cold water, the vinegar, parsley, tarragon, salt, and pepper until smooth.
5. With the motor running, gradually add the olive oil, increasing the flow as the mixture thickens. Turn the blender off and on to mix the ingredients well.
6. Pour ¼ cup of dressing over the vegetables in the bowl and mix together.
7. Arrange vegetables and the raw mushrooms on the lettuce leaves in a basket and serve.

SERVES 6 TO 8. Serving size: ½ cup as a side dish, 1 cup as a main dish.

5 small red potatoes

¼ teaspoon salt

½ pound asparagus (tough ends snapped off)

½ bunch broccoli, cut into small florets

6 small carrots, peeled

10 edible-pod peas, strings removed

6 scallions, including green tops, chopped

½ pound small (1 to 1½-inch diameter) button mushroom caps, cleaned with damp towel

4 or 5 small inner leaves from 1 head of romaine lettuce, washed and crisped by soaking in ice water

Dressing

3 tablespoons white wine vinegar

⅔ cup chopped fresh parsley

1½ teaspoons dried tarragon, crumbled

½ teaspoon salt

¼ teaspoon pepper

1¼ cups olive oil

Pressed Leek, Asparagus, and Zucchini Terrine with Mustard-Lemon Dressing

1½ pounds small to medium leeks

½ teaspoon dried tarragon

1½ cups vegetable stock (not low-sodium)

1 pound zucchini, cut into ½-inch slices

1 pound asparagus, tough ends snapped off

¼ teaspoon salt

Mustard-Lemon Dressing

½ cup olive oil

3 tablespoons lemon juice

1 tablespoon Dijon mustard

¼ teaspoon pepper

Salt to taste

1. Oil the sides and bottom of a 5 × 9-inch loaf pan and set aside together with an unoiled loaf pan the same size.
2. Trim the root ends and tops from the leeks (save 10 tender green inner leaves from the tops), leaving about 1 inch of dark green leaves.
3. Cut the leeks in half lengthwise and rinse under running water, gently separating the layers to remove dirt. Rinse the reserved inner leaves and set the leeks aside.
4. In a 4- to 5-quart pan, bring the tarragon, salt, and stock to a boil over high heat.
5. Add all the leeks, reduce the heat, cover, and simmer until tender when pierced, about 15 minutes. Remove the leeks from the pan and drain, reserving the cooking water.
6. Add the zucchini and asparagus to the pan and let boil for 4 minutes. Remove and drain.
7. Layer the vegetables in the prepared loaf pan, beginning with the leeks, until all the vegetables are in.
8. Set the other loaf pan on top of the vegetables and fill with 4 pounds of weight to weigh them down. Canned goods or dried beans work best.
9. Refrigerate for at least 8 hours or up to 2 days to firm.
10. Prepare the dressing: In a blender, combine the olive oil, lemon juice, mustard, pepper, and salt. Refrigerate until ready to use.
11. When ready to serve the vegetables, remove from the refrigerator and pour off any liquid that has accumulated. Remove the weighted pan, and with a very sharp knife, gently cut the loaf crosswise into 10 slices.
12. Using two spatulas, lift out the slices to a platter or individual salad plates. (Though more difficult to slice, the terrine is handsome inverted onto a platter. Cut carefully.) Top with the dressing and season with salt.

SERVES 6. Serving size: 1½ slices.

Broccoli Piquant

1. Cook the broccoli in a medium skillet according to the package directions.
2. Add the vinegar and garlic to the broccoli, and continue cooking for 10 minutes. Remove the broccoli from the skillet and cut into pieces. Set the broccoli aside.
3. Add the butter to the skillet and heat until melted. Add the breadcrumbs and cook until brown.
4. Pour the breadcrumbs and sauce over the hot broccoli and sprinkle with additional crumbs.

SERVES 2 TO 3. Serving size: ½ cup.

One 10-ounce package frozen broccoli (or use steamed fresh broccoli)

2 tablespoons apple cider vinegar

½ garlic clove, minced

1 tablespoon butter

¼ cup soft breadcrumbs

Roasted Vegetables

1 rutabaga, quartered

2 turnips, halved

1 potato, quartered

3 medium carrots, peeled and halved

4 small white onions, peeled

1 eggplant, peeled and quartered lengthwise

1 zucchini, sliced into ¼-inch rounds

2 yellow squash, sliced into ¼-inch rounds

10 asparagus, tough ends snapped off and discarded

6 broccoli florets

Seasoning

3 packets dried onion soup mix

3 tablespoons extra virgin olive oil

2 tablespoons granulated garlic

1 teaspoon seasoning salt, such as Lawry's

½ teaspoon fresh/ground pepper

1. Grease a large, shallow baking pan.
2. In a large saucepan, bring 1 quart water to a boil over high heat and add the rutabaga, turnips, potato, carrots, and onions. Boil for 4 minutes.
3. Drain and allow to cool for 30 minutes.
4. Preheat the oven to 350°F. Slice the onions into ¼-inch-thick disks, but do not separate the rings.
5. While the vegetables are cooling, prepare the seasoning: In a small bowl, whisk together the soup mix, olive oil, garlic, seasoning salt, and pepper.
6. Rub the seasoning over the eggplant, zucchini, squash, asparagus, broccoli, and boiled vegetables, coating completely, and place in the pan. Layer the onion disks on top.
7. Bake for 35 to 40 minutes, until as brown as desired.

SERVES 4. Serving size: 1 piece of each roasted vegetable.

If you let these vegetables come to room temperature, make a vinaigrette of 2 tablespoons olive oil, 1½ tablespoons balsamic vinegar, and 1 tablespoon water. Mix it well and pour it over the roasted vegetables, and you'll have a dish so delicious it will make portion control a difficult task.

Brussels Sprouts and Mushrooms

1¾ pounds Brussels sprouts (or use two 10-ounce boxes frozen Brussels sprouts)

½ teaspoon salt, or more to taste

3 tablespoons butter

½ pound white button mushrooms, sliced into ¼-inch pieces

1 medium onion, sliced into ¼-inch pieces

1 green bell pepper, sliced into ¼-inch pieces

¼ teaspoon pepper, or more to taste

1. Wash and trim the sprouts. With a sharp knife make an X in the stem of each sprout.
2. Bring 1 cup water to a boil in a saucepan and add the salt. Add the sprouts and cook, uncovered, for 8 to 10 minutes over medium heat.
4. Cover and cook for 10 minutes more or just until crisp-tender. Drain and place the sprouts in a bowl.
5. Meanwhile, in a large skillet, heat the butter and add the mushrooms, onion, and bell pepper. Cook until tender.
6. Add to the sprouts and season with the salt and pepper.

SERVES 4. Serving size: 1 cup as a main dish.

Orange-Stuffed Squash

1. Wash the squash and cut into halves lengthwise. Scoop out the seeds.
2. In a large skillet, lay the cut sides in approximately 1 inch water with ¼ teaspoon salt. Cover and let steam over medium heat for 15 minutes. Drain, pat dry, and remove, cut side up, to a baking dish.
3. Meanwhile, preheat the oven to 400°F.
4. Put 1 teaspoon brown sugar, 1 generous teaspoon butter, and a pinch of salt in the center of each squash half.
5. Place the baking dish in the oven and bake for 15 minutes.
6. While the squash is baking, combine the remaining brown sugar, the oranges, orange juice, and cinnamon in a bowl.
7. Remove the baking dish, place ½ teaspoon of the orange mixture into each squash half, and return to the oven for another 30 minutes.
8. Turn off the oven. Let sit in the cooling oven for 30 minutes. Serve warm.

SERVES 4. **Serving size:** ½ squash.

2 acorn squash (about 2 pounds)

½ teaspoon salt

¼ cup firmly packed brown sugar

1½ tablespoons butter or margarine

2 oranges, peeled and segmented

1 cup store-bought orange juice

1 teaspoon ground cinnamon

Sweet Potatoes McMillan

1. Preheat the oven to 375°F. Butter a 1-quart casserole dish. Melt 2 tablespoons of butter and set aside.
2. Combine the sweet potatoes, 4 tablespoons butter, the sugar, ginger, cinnamon, and salt in a large bowl. Mix well.
3. Stir in the Grand Marnier and milk until fully incorporated.
4. Turn into the prepared casserole dish, brush the top with the melted butter, and sprinkle with the orange zest–sugar mix.
5. Bake for 30 to 40 minutes, until browned.

SERVES 6. Serving size: 2 tablespoons.

Some hosts serve this as a side dish with roasted fresh ham or roasted pork.

6 tablespoons butter or margarine, plus more for pan

4 cups mashed boiled (with skin on) sweet potatoes

¼ cup sugar

¼ teaspoon ground ginger

½ teaspoon ground cinnamon

¼ teaspoon salt

¼ cup Grand Marnier

2 tablespoons milk or light cream

1 tablespoon grated orange zest mixed with 1 tablespoon sugar

A PINT OF SOUP

unt Tee (T for Teresa) was known to be an excellent and generous cook who liked a glass of whiskey from time to time. She used a ploy that rarely failed because she didn't use it too often.

She told me she would cut up an onion and two cloves of garlic and put them in water to boil. When one of her friends came by, she would open the kitchen door and let the aroma invade the living room. The visitor would ask, "What are you cooking, Tee?" Her answer would be "A little bit of this and a little bit of that. But, you know, I am fresh out of bourbon."

That would be the cue for the man to say "I'll go get a pint."

In his absence, Aunt Tee would turn off the pot and close the door. She would bring glasses and ice with her to the cocktail table. The visitor, whose tongue would be dripping at the prospect of a "Teresa meal," would be told, "That pot in there"—pointing to the kitchen—"is preparation for something I am cooking tomorrow."

People in the family laughed at that story for generations. But I did learn that if I was lonely, or had been away from my home for two or three weeks, my house needed the fix of some aromatic promises coming from my kitchen.

I have gone to the stove, without expecting any visitors, and needing no one to bring me whiskey, and whipped up a beef bourguignonne, chicken and dumplings, or just bacon and eggs.

A lonely house—cold and unfriendly, not necessarily in temperature, but in aloofness—is a place offering scant welcome even to its owner.

The kitchen, which may be floor-licking clean, does not promise the passerby delicious concoctions.

When I return home after being away, I follow an unchanging routine that warms my house and makes it happy to have me back. I open the front door, put my luggage down inside, and immediately go to the kitchen. I take an onion and a potato from the pantry. I wash the potato, and peel and slice each vegetable. I put a heavy-bottomed skillet on the stove with one tablespoon vegetable oil and turn the fire to a medium heat. As it heats, I add the sliced vegetables. I don't want to fry them, so I turn down the heat. I add one clove of minced garlic, a package of frozen mixed vegetables, two bay leaves, and two cups of beef stock. I cover the skillet and turn the fire to its lowest number.

Then I take the luggage to the bedroom and leave the door open. As the aromas begin to reach down the hall, I can almost hear the walls and floorboards and carpet hum in preparation for singing a Welcome Home composition.

In the kitchen I remove the cover and let the warm aromatic steam gush forth, moistening my face, neck, and arms. When I have dried myself, I look around. My house is mine again. It is no longer angry with me for leaving it so long, alone so long. I never know exactly what I shall do with the skillet of vegetables, whether it will become a soup, a stew, or just pureed stock for future use.

All I know is my house has forgiven me and taken me safely back into its loving care.

Try this ploy: Whenever the house resists you, the kitchen can be made into your ally. Start there first, and start with soup.

Black Bean Soup

1. Examine the beans, removing any debris, then wash. Soak overnight in cold water to cover.
2. Drain the beans. In a soup kettle or pot put 1 quart of stock, the beans, onions, garlic, ham hock if desired, salt, and pepper.
3. Bring to a boil, then turn the heat down and simmer for about 2 hours, until the beans are very soft and the ham hock, if using, is tender.
4. Remove the skin and bones from the ham hock and place the hock in a blender with 2 to 3 cups of beans. Blend until smooth. Repeat until all the beans are pureed.
5. Return the bean puree to the kettle and simmer for 5 minutes over low heat. Thin with stock or water if necessary.
6. Serve hot, with a dollop of sour cream atop the soup in each bowl. Reheat as a snack anytime.

SERVES 6 TO 8. Serving size: 1 cup.

1 pound dried black beans

3 quarts chicken stock (or vegetable stock if preferred, or water)

1½ medium onions, chopped

1 garlic clove, chopped

1 ham hock (optional)

¼ teaspoon salt

¼ teaspoon pepper

One 8-ounce container sour cream

Chicken Soup

1. Heat the oil in a large skillet. Add the chicken and cook well over medium heat.
2. Combine the chicken, chicken stock, and lemon juice in a large saucepan. Add the salt and pepper and simmer for 20 minutes.
3. Add the zucchini, squash, green beans, and asparagus. Cook for 20 minutes.

SERVES 4. Serving size: 1 cup of soup.

1½ tablespoons vegetable oil

1⅓ cups diced skinless chicken

1 quart chicken stock

⅔ teaspoon lemon juice

⅓ teaspoon salt

¼ teaspoon pepper

¼ cup diced zucchini

¼ cup diced yellow squash

¼ cup diced green beans

¼ cup diced asparagus

One steaming bowl of chicken soup will be a wonderful way to break your fast in the morning. Also, roasted vegetables (page 96) work deliciously in this soup. Use them in place of the zucchini, squash, green beans, and asparagus.

Pumpkin Soup I

2 tablespoons (¼ stick) butter

2 tablespoons all-purpose flour

2½ cups milk

¼ teaspoon ground cinnamon

¼ teaspoon ground nutmeg

½ teaspoon salt

¼ cup firmly packed brown sugar

2 cups canned pumpkin puree

1 quart vegetable stock

2 egg yolks, beaten

1. Melt the butter in a large saucepan.
2. Blend in the flour, using a whisk.
3. Over low heat, slowly add the milk, a little at a time, stirring constantly until the mixture is a smooth sauce.
4. Combine the cinnamon, nutmeg, salt, brown sugar, and pumpkin in a large bowl. Mix well and add to the saucepan.
5. Add the vegetable stock and simmer for 5 minutes.
6. Temper the eggs by pouring a little of the hot liquid into them. Mix well and pour the eggs into the soup. Simmer for 5 minutes.

SERVES 6. Serving size: 1 bowl.

Pumpkin Soup II

1. Preheat the oven to 350°F.
2. Split the pumpkin in half. Remove the seeds and save them.
3. Put both pumpkin halves, cut side down, in a deep broiling pan with ½ inch of water. Bake for 40 minutes.
4. While the pumpkin is cooking, thoroughly wash the seeds. Pat dry and sprinkle with salt. Toast the seeds in the vegetable oil in a hot skillet and set aside.
5. Remove the pumpkin from the oven and let cool. When cool enough to handle, scoop out the meat into a large bowl, about 2 cups. Freeze any leftovers in 4 portions for use later.
6. Put the milk, vegetable stock, and pumpkin in a medium saucepan and heat, mixing thoroughly, until all the ingredients are blended.
7. Serve hot. Sprinkle on the cinnamon and to each bowl add a spoonful of sour cream and a few sprinkles of toasted seeds.

SERVES 4. Serving size: 1 cup.

1 large pumpkin (about 3 pounds)

2 tablespoons vegetable oil

1¼ cups milk

2 cups vegetable stock

¼ teaspoon ground cinnamon

One 8-ounce container sour cream

I often make this soup from scratch during October, when pumpkins are available everywhere.

 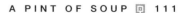

Consommé Double

2 quarts store-bought
  chicken stock

1 medium onion, diced

2 celery stalks

3 garlic cloves

2 bay leaves

4 pounds chicken backs and
  necks, fresh or frozen

1. Fill a generous pot with the chicken stock and 1 quart water. Add the onion, celery, garlic, and bay leaves. Boil for 20 to 25 minutes.

2. Put the pieces of chicken, fresh or frozen, into the stock. Boil vigorously for 1 hour.

3. Take the pot off the stove and let the contents cool.

4. Skim off any scum at the top, then strain the broth. (I pour it through a four-ply cheesecloth in a strainer.)

5. Place the strained broth in the freezer in 6 small packets (1½ cups per packet) so the entire batch does not have to be defrosted.

SERVES 6. Serving size: 1 cup.

This broth is made even better if you can use the frozen necks, gizzards, and livers from turkeys that you have roasted. Because we are starting with chicken stock instead of water and making the stock much stronger by cooking it with pieces of poultry, the broth is called a consommé double.

TIP

Refrigerator Soup

When I want to warm up my house, perk up my personality, and most in general give myself a feeling of good time, I have often gone to my refrigerator and made a refrigerator soup.

The ingredients are a compilation of anything edible that will fit into a pot and will go with my frozen poultry stock.

A pot of aromatic soup is great ammunition against depression.

THIS WINTER DAY

The kitchen is its readiness
white green and orange things
leak their blood selves in the soup.

Ritual sacrifice that snaps
an odor at my nose and starts
my tongue to march,
slipping in the liquid of its drip.

The day, silver striped
in rain, is balked against
my window and the soup.

OUR DAILY BREAD

S tolen waters are sweet, and bread eaten in secret is pleasant." So we are told in the Book of Proverbs in the King James Version of the Holy Bible. I know that bread eaten in secret can be wonderful. But if you eat enough, it will be a secret no longer.

I had a family member who was gentle and soft-spoken, with the patience of Job. However, if his wife set the table without putting bread on it, he lost his pretty ways. He would shout, knock the table, and stomp his feet until she placated him with a pan of biscuits, a skillet of corn bread, or a sliced loaf of white bread.

In Proverbs 23:2, we are advised to ". . . put a knife to thy throat if thou be a person given to appetite." I do not quite agree that one has to be quite so harsh, but I do know that if you want to be svelte and remain that way, control your appetite in the eating of bread. So, I would advise you to eat one piece of bread with the first serving of a dish, and none when you go back for snacks.

Popovers

1. Preheat the oven to 425°F. Grease six custard cups or an iron popover pan.
2. Beat the eggs slightly in a large bowl.
3. Add the milk and butter, then add the flour and salt. Beat vigorously for 2 minutes.
4. Pour the batter into very hot custard cups or iron popover pans, filling two-thirds full. Place in the oven and bake for about 40 minutes or until fully risen and brown.
5. Serve at once.

SERVES 6. Serving size: 1 popover with omelet, or 2 plain popovers.

2 eggs

1 cup milk

2 tablespoons (¼ stick) butter, melted

1 cup sifted all-purpose flour

¼ teaspoon salt

If you plan to serve the popovers later, open each popover, place a little savory egg-and-ham omelet inside, and reheat.

TIP

Biscuit Quick

When making homemade biscuits, I sift all my dry ingredients together, and then cut the shortening into the mix until it resembles coarse cornmeal. I put it into a zippered bag and into the freezer, where it can stay for up to one year.

When I'm ready to serve biscuits, I take out 2¼ cups of the dry mixture and add 1 cup of milk. I roll it on a floured board and cut out biscuits as I desire.

This tip has saved me a lot of time and some anxiety about getting flour on my clothes, or on my face, or on the floor just as I am about to serve.

Buttermilk Biscuits

From *Hallelujah! The Welcome Table*

4 cups all-purpose flour

½ teaspoon salt

6 teaspoons baking powder

1 teaspoon baking soda

1 cup lard

2 cups buttermilk

All-purpose flour

1. Preheat the oven to 375°F.
2. Sift the flour with the salt, baking powder, and baking soda. Cut in the lard until the mixture resembles coarse cornmeal. Add the buttermilk, and stir until the dough leaves the sides of the bowl.
3. Turn the dough out onto a lightly floured board and knead until smooth. Roll out to a ½-inch thickness and cut into 2-inch rounds. If there is no biscuit cutter at hand, use a water glass. (Turn glass upside down, dust rim in flour, and cut biscuits.)
4. Bake on an ungreased cookie sheet for 20 to 25 minutes, until the biscuits are golden brown.

MAKES 2 DOZEN BISCUITS

Serving size: 1 biscuit

Orange Nut Bread

1. Grease a 9 × 5 × 3-inch loaf pan with shortening.
2. Sift the flour, baking powder, salt, and sugar into a large bowl.
3. Cut in the shortening with a pastry blender, two knives, or your fingers until the ingredients are about the size of green peas.
4. Add the milk, orange juice, and egg, mixing only enough to dampen the flour mixture.
5. Stir in the grated rind and nuts, being careful not to over-mix.
6. Pour into the prepared loaf pan, spreading the batter to the corners and leaving a slight depression in the center. Let stand for 20 minutes.
7. Meanwhile, preheat the oven to 350°F.
8. Bake for about 1 hour or until the top is golden and a knife inserted into the center of the bread comes out clean.
9. Let stand for 5 minutes, then invert onto a rack to cool.
10. Store overnight in the icebox before slicing.

SERVES 8. Serving size: 1 slice.

¼ cup vegetable shortening, plus more for pan

2½ cups all-purpose flour

2 teaspoons baking powder

½ teaspoon salt

1 cup sugar

¾ cup milk

¼ cup fresh orange juice

1 egg

1 tablespoon grated orange rind

1 cup chopped nuts

Enjoy with tea or coffee at any time, day or night.

Corn Sticks

¼ cup melted shortening or
  vegetable oil, plus more for
  pans
½ cup all-purpose flour
1 cup yellow cornmeal
1 teaspoon baking powder
½ teaspoon salt
1 teaspoon sugar
1 egg, beaten
½ cup milk

Serve with mixed green salad or as a snack with a bowl of hot chicken broth. Enjoy one!

1. Preheat the oven to 450°F. Grease cast iron corn stick pans.
2. Sift together the flour, cornmeal, baking powder, salt, and sugar.
3. Add the egg, milk, and melted shortening or oil, stirring until just blended. Mix only enough to dampen the cornmeal mixture.
4. Heat the greased corn stick pans in the oven for 20 minutes.
5. Pour in the batter and bake for about 30 minutes or until done and beautifully brown. Pierce 1 corn stick with a toothpick. If toothpick comes out clean, the bread is done.

SERVES 4. Serving size: 1 corn stick.

Orange Syrup for Waffles, Pancakes, or Toast

2 cups orange juice

½ cup honey

2 tablespoons (¼ stick) butter

1. Boil the orange juice in a medium saucepan and reduce it to 1 cup.
2. Add the honey and butter. Stir well until all the ingredients are blended.
3. Pour over pancakes, griddle cakes, waffles, or pastries for a company-pleasing trimming.

Makes about 1½ cups.

All Day and All Night Corn Bread

3 tablespoons butter

½ cup all-purpose flour

1½ cups white cornmeal

2 tablespoons sugar

1 teaspoon salt

1 tablespoon baking powder

1½ cups plus 2 tablespoons milk

1 egg, well beaten

1. Preheat the oven to 400°F. Melt the butter in an 8-inch square pan.
2. Sift together the flour, cornmeal, sugar, salt, and baking powder into a large bowl.
3. Stir in 1 cup plus 2 tablespoons of the milk and the egg, mixing only enough to dampen the cornmeal mixture.
4. Pour the batter into the pan. Pour the remaining ½ cup milk over the batter and stir.
5. Bake for 35 to 45 minutes, until the top is golden and a toothpick inserted into the center of the bread comes out clean.

SERVES 9. Serving size: 1 square.

When the corn bread has cooled, one 2-inch square can be removed. Open the square horizontally so there is a top and a bottom. Put in one slice of Swiss cheese or Monterey Jack cheese and warm in a toaster oven. Serve for breakfast with the hot beverage of your choice.

LETTUCE PRAISE SALADS

The Presiding Elder—his title is spoken of in ALL CAPS—is, in the Methodist Church, a man of great stature, whether he is a six-footer with great confidence and a booming voice or he is a short roly-poly person with charming ways and a melodious voice.

In Arkansas, where I was growing up under the care of my loving paternal grandmother and her other son, my Uncle Willie, the Presiding Elder's visit was heralded almost as a holiday, no matter that such visits were part of his formal responsibilities, to be done once every three months at each of the churches under his charge. He would preach a fiery sermon, go over the books with the church trustees and preacher, give pep talks to the usher board, and have a glorious scrumptious dinner, always cooked by my grandmother. It was on one of his visits that I began a lifelong love affair with salad.

One Sunday morning, the Presiding Elder had preached until you could smell the very embers of hell burning for those who had disobeyed the church teachings. And those who had been obedient servants could hear the bell—like sounds of the angels' choir—singing "Welcome home, welcome, Christians. You have done well. Welcome, welcome to the Golden Streets of Heaven; you have done well!" Anyway, all of the adults were under his spell, but the children had to use incredible control to keep from laughing at his lugubrious speech and his large unattractive belly.

For the dinner following this sermon, my grandmother had cooked a ham and some large fluffy biscuits and fried a chicken to its golden promising end. She had made a potato salad, and to decorate the dish, she halved more hard-boiled eggs than usual and placed some of them on top, pushing many more down into the salad.

We grew lettuce, which never formed a ball; its leaves were wide, flat, and tender. I had washed the lettuce and my brother Bailey had crushed ice and we put it into my grandmother's crystal bowl. The common way of eating potato salad showed a diner laying one leaf of lettuce onto a salad plate. Then one to two spoons of potato salad would be placed in the center of the salad leaf.

That particular Sunday, the Presiding Elder blessed the table and I thought that he thought he was again in the pulpit, preaching another long-winded sermon. I peeked out of half-closed eyes and saw the ham fat had turned white on the platter and my grandmother's beautiful biscuits, so fluffy earlier, had sat down on themselves. When he finally finished saying the blessing, he looked over the chicken and took two of the largest pieces. He chose the thickest slab of ham, and then he attacked the potato salad. He raked about four halves of the eggs on top and then put a mound of potato salad on the plate, which was already about to collapse.

Bailey saw that—in fact, we all saw that—but Bailey was first. He took the fork from the salad bowl and instead of taking one leaf of lettuce, he put the fork down until he reached the bottom of the bowl and he picked up every leaf and shook them and put them all on his plate. My grandmother looked at him and at his action and said nothing. My Uncle Willie said nothing. The preacher was already eating.

Bailey looked at me; I was mute with fear, so he took the fork and started to put the lettuce back into the bowl. My grandmother in her soft, firm voice said, "No, little mister, you will eat every one of those leaves." Bailey looked at me again and he raked off one leaf into his lap and rolled it as if it was a cigarette under the table and gave it to me to eat, raked another, rolled it, and ate it. Each time Bailey reached for a piece of chicken, my grandmother said, "No, little mister, finish your lettuce first." He and I ate every shred of lettuce and my grandmother excused us from the table. We cried and laughed. We were angry and tickled.

When the Presiding Elder had left, my grandmother called Bailey and me back to the dining room. She said, "You know there is always something in the kitchen for Grandmother and her children. I would never let that greedy vulture eat everything. You also must know, for every action you also must pay. Now look in the icebox and bring that salad out here."

Warm Garden Salad

1. Blanch the broccoli, asparagus, leeks, rutabaga, mushrooms, and zucchini in boiling water for 5 minutes. Drain and set aside, keeping warm.
2. Prepare the vinaigrette: In a blender, combine the garlic, vinegar, olive oil, sherry, and mustard. Add salt and pepper to taste and puree.
3. Moisten the vegetables with the vinaigrette and arrange on top of the salad greens.

SERVES 6. Serving size: 1 or 2 pieces of each vegetable on a bed of greens.

8 small broccoli florets

8 asparagus tips

4 small leeks, washed thoroughly

1 small rutabaga, cut into thin strips

2 portobello mushrooms, thinly sliced

2 zucchini, thinly sliced

4 cups assorted salad greens or 6 romaine lettuce leaves

Vinaigrette

1 garlic clove, crushed

⅔ cup apple cider vinegar

⅓ cup olive oil

2 tablespoons sherry

⅔ teaspoon prepared mustard (any kind will do)

Salt and pepper

You can return to this dish as often as you choose.

Cold Potato Salad

From *Hallelujah! The Welcome Table*

6 cups cooked potatoes,
  peeled and diced

1 medium onion, finely chopped

1 cup finely diced celery

1 cup chopped dill pickles

1 cup sweet relish, drained

8 large hard-boiled eggs,
  4 chopped, 4 whole

Salt and black pepper

1½ cups mayonnaise

Fresh parsley, chopped

1. Combine the potatoes, onion, celery, pickles, relish, and chopped eggs. Season with salt and pepper, and add the mayonnaise. Chill for several hours.
2. Just before serving, halve the remaining 4 eggs and place them on the salad as decoration. Dust the salad with chopped parsley and serve at once.

SERVES 6 TO 8

Serving size: 2 heaping tablespoons.

Chicken-and-Pineapple Salad

1. Dice the chicken and pineapple into large pieces.
2. Stir the vinegar, sugar, and mayonnaise together in a large bowl until the sugar is dissolved. Add the chicken and pineapple.
3. Add the mint to taste and stir well. Serve atop lettuce leaves and sprinkle cashews over the salad, if desired.

SERVES 4 OR 5. Serving size: 2 heaping tablespoons.

2 cooked, skinned chicken breast halves (about 2 pounds)

4 slices ripe pineapple

½ cup rice vinegar or white wine vinegar

2 tablespoons sugar (½ cup if using wine vinegar)

¼ cup mayonnaise

Fresh mint, chopped

Lettuce leaves, crisped by soaking in ice water

½ cup cashew nuts, broken, toasted (optional)

Fruit Mélange

One 8-ounce can pitted dark sweet cherries (water packed), drained

1¼ cups fresh strawberries

1 cantaloupe, cut into balls (about 2½ cups)

1 cup pineapple chunks, drained

½ cup low-sugar orange marmalade

3 teaspoons finely chopped candied ginger

½ ripe banana, sliced

6 fresh mint leaves

1. Chill a large glass serving bowl.
2. Layer the fruit in the chilled bowl, beginning with the cherries and moving on to the strawberries, cantaloupe, and pineapple.
3. In a separate bowl, combine the orange marmalade, ¼ cup hot water, and the candied ginger to create a sauce.
4. Drizzle the orange marmalade sauce over the fruit and chill for 2 hours before serving.
5. When ready to serve, arrange the banana slices on top of the fruit and garnish with the mint leaves.

SERVES 6. **Serving size: 1½ cups.**

To keep the banana from darkening, dip in ascorbic-acid color keeper, such as Fruit-Fresh, or lemon juice mixed with a little water.

Corn Salad

Combine all the ingredients in a large bowl.

SERVES 6. Serving size: ½ cup.

½ cup diced pimiento

1 roasted green bell pepper, peeled, seeded, and diced (about ½ cup)

5 green scallion tops, chopped

1 fresh tomato, seeded, finely diced, and squeezed (about 1 cup)

¼ cup fresh lemon juice

1 tablespoon extra virgin olive oil

One 15-ounce can chickpeas, drained and rinsed

3 cups frozen corn, blanched in simmering water for 3 minutes, drained, then immersed in ice water and drained

1 tablespoon honey mustard

½ teaspoon salt

¼ teaspoon pepper

Chicken-and-Peaches Salad

2 boneless, skinless chicken breasts, cooked and chilled

One 3-ounce package Neufchâtel cheese, at room temperature

¼ cup mayonnaise

1 teaspoon chopped fresh basil leaves

½ teaspoon salt

¼ teaspoon white pepper

One 16-ounce can peach halves (juice packed), drained and diced

½ cup cashews, broken, toasted

½ cup chopped celery

4 lettuce leaves

1. Cube the chicken.
2. Combine the cheese, mayonnaise, basil, salt, and pepper in a large bowl.
3. Add the chicken, peaches, cashews, and celery, and toss well.
4. Chill in the refrigerator for 1 hour. When ready to serve, spoon the salad onto the lettuce leaves.

SERVES 4. Serving size: 2 heaping tablespoons.

If you are eating alone, eat sparingly and return to the salad as frequently as you desire.

SWEET ENDINGS

If you find honey, eat just enough.

—*Proverbs 25:16*

Whether speaking of honey or butter or ice cream, or anything, it is wise to eat just enough. You are going to be overjoyed when you manage your portions—even if just for two weeks.

Crème Caramel

1. Scald the milk with the vanilla in a large saucepan over low heat. Remove from the heat and let sit, covered, for 30 minutes.

2. In a separate saucepan, prepare caramel for an 8-cup mold: Combine 3 tablespoons water, the lemon juice, and ½ cup sugar and cook over medium-high heat until golden. Watch carefully that it doesn't become too dark and burn, as it may taste bitter.

3. Carefully pour the caramel into the mold, tilting the mold to fully coat the bottom and sides. Let sit until the caramel hardens, about 2 minutes.

4. Preheat the oven to 300°F.

5. Whisk together the eggs, yolks, the remaining 1 cup sugar, and the salt in a large bowl until the mixture is pale yellow and thick enough to coat a spoon or spatula.

6. Pour the scalded milk mixture into the egg mixture and mix well with a wooden spoon to make a custard.

7. Using a fine metal kitchen strainer, carefully strain the custard mixture into the caramelized mold.

8. Place the mold in a larger pan more than 1 inch deep. Set the larger pan on an oven shelf, and fill with at least 1 inch of water, until it comes halfway up the mold.

9. Bake for 60 to 75 minutes, until the custard is set. (You'll know it's ready when a knife inserted in the center comes out clean.) Remove the pan and mold from the oven and set the mold outside the larger pan to cool for 2 hours.

10. Refrigerate for at least 8 hours, or overnight. When ready to serve, run a knife around the edges of the mold. Cover the mold with a deep serving dish and overturn the mold. Allow the caramel to coat the custard. Cut into portions before serving, then serve some of the crème caramel with cream.

SERVES 6. Serving size: ½ cup.

1 quart milk

1 teaspoon pure vanilla extract

⅛ teaspoon lemon juice or vinegar

1½ cups sugar

8 large eggs

4 large egg yolks

Pinch of salt

The long, slow cooking of this classic dessert produces a perfectly smooth and silky custard.

Pears in Port Wine

4 ripe, firm pears

3 cups ruby port wine

¼ cup sugar

1 jigger (3 tablespoons) Cointreau

2 teaspoons pure vanilla extract

1. Peel the pears, but leave them whole. With the stem end intact, cut off a thin slice at the bottom so that the pears can stand upright.

2. In a nonreactive saucepan, bring the port, sugar, and 2 cups water to a boil.

3. Place the whole pears in the liquid, lower the heat, and simmer, uncovered, for about 35 minutes, turning the pears occasionally, until they are tender.

4. Remove the pears with a slotted spoon and set aside to cool.

5. Increase the heat under the saucepan and reduce the liquid by half by boiling vigorously for 20 minutes to a medium-thick syrup. Add the Cointreau and vanilla.

6. Place the pears upright in a serving dish and spoon the reduced syrup over them. Chill for at least 2 hours before serving.

SERVES 4. Serving size: 1 pear, or if half a pear will satisfy, offer vanilla ice cream at the first serving.

Second and third servings could be eaten in the morning with
coffee or in the afternoon with a cup of aromatic tea.

TIP

Raise a Glass

White wines such as Chardonnay, Chablis, and Riesling must be served cold. I have not said U.S. wines are the best, but they are my favorites.

Fortunately, there are American wines as tasty as any wine in the world and thankfully less expensive. I serve California, Washington State, and New York wines and have always been pleased with my guests' reception of my choice.

Red wines such as Cabernet Sauvignon, Merlot, Bordeaux, and Pinot Noir are easily found in your local wine store. Some need to be decanted, especially the older, bigger red wines. I encourage you to pour the red wine you are going to serve into a decanter, two hours before dinner, to achieve its optimum flavor.

Some guests still drink sherry. I serve Dry Sack and cocktail sherry before meals and sometimes a good port after dinner. And a generous host provides Grand Marnier, Cointreau, Baileys, Frangelico, and other cognacs and brandies to please the guests.

It must be remembered that a good friend does not allow a guest to drive after too much alcohol. So have a good time and be wise.

Party Hearty

In my early teens, my paternal grandmother brought my brother and me from a dusky little village in Arkansas to live with our mother in San Francisco. The big streets, fast cars, my mother, who wore makeup, and white teachers and students in school frightened me. I wanted to be friendly at least with the other African Americans, but I was too terrified to talk. My fast-talking, brilliant brother made friends immediately, but I closed myself off and became lonelier.

At school, the girls would talk about boys and parties and good times. They did not try to prevent me from hearing them. Finally I went to my mother and told her how lonely I was and that the other girls gave parties where they had fun, but no one invited me. She gave me some advice, which I have used forever. She said, "If someone draws a circle and leaves you out, you draw a bigger circle and include them in it. If they have not invited you to their parties—you invite them to yours."

She encouraged me to go to the five and ten cents store and buy invitations and then write, "Maya invites you to a birthday party. Although it is nobody's birthday that we know, we will have spaghetti with large meatballs, garlic toast of sourdough bread, all the salad you can eat, a massive cake, good music and dancing. Please respond."

I offered ten invitations. Twenty people answered. Some girls brought boys. I was afraid my mother would not want boys and girls in her beautiful house. "They will be all right," she said. "I will cook all the food, Papa Ford will serve buffet style, and I will be here in the house. I will walk through no more than three times. Don't worry—they will behave and you will give a great party."

In my fifties, I moved to North Carolina from California. I already had some fame, but no one invited me to anything, so I had some invitations printed saying, "Maya Angelou invites you to a 'Welcome to Spring Party.' We will have laughter, good food, some dancing, some drinking, and some story-telling." I invited twenty people, remembering what had happened the first time. I prepared for forty and that's how many came. I do not suggest that there are recipes in this book that will help you to make new friends, but I assure you they will introduce you to people you have never heard of.

Happy Cooking and Happy Eating, all day and all night long.

Acknowledgments

I am indebted to Robert Loomis and Porscha Burke of Random House. They demonstrated exquisite patience with me as I slow-crawled through this manuscript.

I am indebted to my late mother for leaving me memories of great food for use all my life long. My indebtedness to M.F.K. Fisher is enormous. From her I learned to be bold in the kitchen but never casual. I learned that the cook may shock but must never be careless.

To Chef Don McMillan and every good cook who dared to serve great tamales, fried chicken, wonton soup, roast beef with Yorkshire pudding, and pasta primavera . . . thank you.

Index

About the Author

Poet, writer, performer, teacher, and director MAYA ANGELOU was raised in Stamps, Arkansas, and then went to San Francisco. In addition to her bestselling autobiographies, beginning with *I Know Why the Caged Bird Sings,* she has also written five poetry collections, including *I Shall Not Be Moved* and *Shaker, Why Don't You Sing?,* and a cookbook, *Hallelujah! The Welcome Table,* as well as the celebrated poem "On the Pulse of Morning," which she read at the inauguration of President William Jefferson Clinton, and "A Brave and Startling Truth," written at the request of the United Nations and read at its fiftieth anniversary. She lives in Winston-Salem, North Carolina.

About the Text

This book was set in Bembo, a typeface based on an old-style Roman face that was used for Cardinal Bembo's tract *De Aetna* in 1495. Bembo was cut by Francisco Griffo in the early sixteenth century. The Lanston Monotype Machine Company of Philadelphia brought the well-proportioned letter forms of Bembo to the United States in the 1930s.